LOIRE V WINE REGIONS

A Connoisseurs Guide to History, Grape Varieties, Flavors and Wine Regions of Loire Valley

By

Lucien C. Deschamps

COPYRIGHT

Copyright ©2024 Lucien C. Deschamps

All rights reserved. No portion of this work may be duplicated without the author's express written consent, whether through mechanical, electronic, or information storage and retrieval techniques.

This book's content is meant to be used only educationally; it is not meant to take the place of professional wine experts' guidance. Any losses or damages resulting from using the information in this book are not covered by the publisher or author.

TABLE OF CONTENTS

Introduction	3
Loire Valley Geography	6
Loire Valley History	9
Loire Valley Viticulture	12
Major Grape Varieties	21
Wine Regions	36
Anjou Region	36
Auvergne Region	84
Crémant de Loire Region	99
Pays Nantais Region	102
Touraine Region	125
Upper Loire Region	162
Vendée-Poitou Region	195
Vendômois Region	206
50 Loire Wine Brand And Regions	215
Loire Wine And Their Food Pairing	218

Introduction

The Loire Valley, located in central France along the gorgeous banks of the Loire River, is a monument to the artistry of winemaking and the unique terroir that creates its wines. This historic region, known as the Garden of France, is not only a treasure trove of architectural masterpieces but also a nursery of exquisite wines that reflect centuries of tradition and creativity.

The Loire Valley's winemaking history extends back to the Roman Empire, and its vines cover more than 185,000 acres, creating a complex tapestry of varieties that thrive in its peculiar temperature and soil. The valley's terroir, defined by a mosaic of microclimates, runs from a cool Atlantic-influenced temperature in the west to a warmer continental climate in the east, making it a perfect canvas for a broad range of grape varietals.

Sauvignon Blanc, Chenin Blanc, Cabernet Franc, and Gamay are among the main grape varieties grown in the region, each expressing itself distinctively among the numerous Loire Valley appellations. Loire Valley wines represent the creative marriage of grape to terroir, from the crisp, minerally Sauvignon Blancs of Sancerre to the honeyed richness of Vouvray's Chenin Blanc and the beautiful reds of Chinon's Cabernet Franc.

The Loire Valley is a living museum of French history and culture beyond the grapes. Majestic châteaux dot the countryside, and the Renaissance influence may be seen in the architecture of small villages and enormous estates. Beyond the vineyards, the cultural significance of Loire Valley wines pervades art, literature, and local traditions.

This introduction takes us on a tour through terroir-rich vineyards, delves into the intricacies of grape varietals, and delves into the cultural tapestry that weaves together the past, present, and future of Loire Valley wines.

Loire Valley Geography

The Loire Valley, which stretches for 280 kilometers (170 miles), is a valley in central France that is divided into the administrative regions Pays de la Loire & Centre-Val de Loire. The Loire Valley is approximately 800 square kilometers (310 square miles) in size.It is renowned as the Cradle of the French and the Garden of France because of the abundance of vineyards, fruit orchards (such as cherries), artichoke, and asparagus fields that line the river's banks. The valley, which has been inhabited since the Middle Paleolithic period, is famous for its medieval cities, architecture, and wines. The oldest documented Neanderthal engravings stretch back to over 57,000 years and were unearthed in an underground chamber in La Roche-Cotard. In 2000, UNESCO added the central Loire River valley to its collection of World Heritage Sites.

The Loire Valley, also known as the "Garden of France. This charming region is known for its breathtaking vistas, old châteaux, and, of course, its world-class wines. The Loire Valley's geography is crucial in producing the specific characteristics of its wines.

The Loire River, which flows through a variety of topographies, from rolling hills to limestone plateaus, influences the valley's unique terroir. Vineyards are grown on both the north and south banks of the river, with each area contributing distinct characteristics to the wines produced. Northern vineyards, for example, have a milder climate, which encourages the development of grape varietals like Sauvignon Blanc and results in crisp, aromatic whites like those found in the Sancerre and Pouilly-Fumé appellations.

The climate of the Loire Valley is classed as temperate marine, with pleasant temperatures and moderate rainfall. The vineyards in the region benefit from the Atlantic Ocean's influence, which reduces dramatic temperature changes. This climate is ideal for growing a wide variety of grape varietals, each of which thrives in its own microclimate. Chenin Blanc, for example, thrives in the somewhat warmer climate of Vouvray, producing exquisite and age-worthy white wines.

Furthermore, the temperature of the Loire Valley encourages the production of red wines, with Cabernet Franc prospering in the region's somewhat warmer areas. Elevation and soil composition variations add to the richness of Loire Valley wines, resulting in a tapestry of flavors that reflect the terroir of each appellation.

Loire Valley History

The Loire Valley, in the heart of France, has a rich historical tapestry that effortlessly intertwines with its famed winemaking culture. The region's historical significance attests to the lasting attractiveness of its landscapes, castles, and vineyards.

The Loire Valley has been a favorite haunt of French kings and nobility since the Middle Ages. The valley's strategic location acted as an important crossroads and natural barrier, defining the region's future. The enormous châteaux dotting the landscape are architectural marvels as well as emblems of authority. Iconic castles like Château de Chambord and Château de Chenonceau not only embody the region's luxury, but they have also witnessed crucial episodes in French history.

The Loire Valley was a center of cultural and intellectual interchange throughout the Renaissance. Poets, philosophers, and artists were drawn to the royal court's sponsorship of the arts, creating a milieu of creativity that left an everlasting stamp on the region's identity. The marriage of creative expression and viticulture established the Loire Valley's image as the "Garden of France."

The Loire Valley saw a viticultural renaissance in the nineteenth century. Many of France's vineyards were destroyed by the phylloxera pandemic, requiring a change in winemaking processes. With its unique geography and grape varietals, the Loire has grown as a resilient and adaptable wine area. Chenin Blanc, Sauvignon Blanc, and Cabernet Franc cultivation developed, establishing the Loire Valley as a prominent player in the world of wine.

The Loire Valley's historical significance extends beyond its regal past. During World War II, the region was a vital center of the French Resistance, with its underground caves providing safe havens for precious art and as a haven for individuals fleeing persecution.

Today, tourists to the Loire Valley are not just experiencing a wine region; they are stepping into a living history of France. The vineyards, châteaux, and ancient cellars echo the footsteps of kings, the murmurs of poets, and the tenacity of winemakers, collectively chronicling this magnificent region's enduring historical narrative.

Loire Valley Viticulture

The Loire Valley covers more than 185,000 acres (750 km2) and is almost two-thirds the size of the Bordeaux wine area. The location and marginal climate of the region mean that the quality of a vintage has a significant impact on the overall quality of the wines produced there, even more so than in other French wine regions. The most frequent risk is that the cool weather will keep the grapes from reaching full ripeness and generating the sugar content required to counteract the high acidity of the grapes. The wines made from Sauvignon blanc have more noticeable mineral notes, are lighter in color, and are less fruity during these chilly vintages. The Cabernet Franc-based wines smell more like "weed" or vegetables and have lighter colors. Raspberries and lead pencil shavings can be detected in the scents of a Loire Cabernet franc in richer vintages.

The average number of vines planted in the Loire Valley is 1,600–2,000 vines per acre, or 4,000–5,000 per hectare. There are as many as 10,000 plants per hectare in some Sancerre vineyards. In order to offset the excessive yields that certain grape varieties, such as Chenin blanc, are known to have, the density of the vines is intended to increase competition for the same few resources found in the soil. Crop management and pruning have become more effective means of limiting output in recent decades.

Malolactic fermentation and barrel aging are generally avoided while making wine in the Loire. Nonetheless, a few vintners have started experimenting with both. Here, chaptalization is allowed and can assist winemakers in making up for under ripe grapes in certain years. In order to enhance the color and tannin content of red wines, there has been a greater focus on prolonging the skin contact maceration period. Controlling the temperature is also crucial because the chilly autumnal weather occasionally needs heating in order to finish the fermentation process completely.

Loire Valley Climate

The Loire River has a considerable impact on the region's microclimate, adding the required few degrees of warmth to allow grapes to develop when the areas to both the north and the south of the Loire Valley have been shown to be hostile to viticulture.

The Loire Valley's environment is crucial in developing the distinct qualities of its wines, adding to the region's status as one of France's best wine-producing regions. The Loire Valley, located in central France, has a temperate marine climate with substantial changes from east to west. The Atlantic Ocean has a strong influence on the climate, resulting in a variety of microclimates along the Loire River.

The climate is more marine in the western Loire Valley, closer to the coast, and is softened by the warming effect of the water. As a result, winters are warmer and summers are colder, great circumstances for developing crisp and fragrant white wines. Sauvignon Blanc, the region's trademark grape, flourishes in these conditions, notably in appellations such as Sancerre and Pouilly-Fumé, where it exhibits its distinctive lively acidity and lemony aromas.

As one travels north towards the eastern regions, the climate becomes more continental, with bigger seasonal temperature changes. This adjustment improves conditions for red grape types like Cabernet Franc. The grape ripens slowly, generating complexity and exquisite tannins, particularly in the Chinon and Bourgueil appellations.

The unique terroir of the Loire Valley, along with the moderating influence of the river and the Atlantic, allows for the growth of a diverse range of grape types. Winemakers select vineyard locations deliberately based on these climatic subtleties, leveraging the distinct conditions to produce a range of wines, from fresh Muscadet in the west to complex reds in the east.

While the overall environment is favorable for wine production, the region faces climate change challenges. Winters are becoming milder, changing traditional frost patterns, and longer growing seasons can affect ripening. To react to these changes, winemakers in the Loire Valley are progressively embracing sustainable techniques, assuring the continuous excellence and diversity of their wines.

Loire Valley Soil

The Loire Valley's soil types play an important influence in developing the specific character and individuality of the wines produced in this renowned French wine area. The varied terroirs created by soil composition changes contribute to the complexity and distinctiveness of the wines developed across the valley's appellations.

Kimmeridgian limestone is a common soil type in the Loire Valley, particularly in the vineyards of Sancerre and Pouilly-Fumé. This old marine sediment gives the Sauvignon Blanc grapes cultivated here a particular minerality, resulting in wines with crisp acidity and a characteristic flinty character. The influence of Kimmeridgian limestone is most visible in the chalky soils, which encourage good drainage, forcing the vines to dig deeper for nutrients and producing grapes with concentrated tastes.

Various soil types contribute to the diversity of Loire Valley wines in the center region of Touraine. The vineyards of Vouvray, where Chenin Blanc thrives, are dominated by clay and limestone soils. These soils retain moisture, ensuring a continuous water supply for the vines while also adding a mineral character to the wines. The grape variety and soil composition combine to produce Vouvrays with a distinct balance of acidity, sweetness, and complexity.

Tuffeau, a soft, porous limestone, characterizes the terroir of the Anjou and Saumur areas. This subsurface soil type provides great drainage and lends a subtle minerality to the Cabernet Franc and Chenin Blanc grapes cultivated here. These wines exhibit a perfect mix of fruit expression and delicate earthiness.

The Loire Valley's commitment to expressing terroir via its wines is obvious in the meticulous selection of grape varieties and production practices that appreciate soil variety. Finally, the Loire Valley soils contribute greatly to the exquisite and varied character of the wines that have given the region its prestigious reputation in the world of winemaking.

Major Grape Varieties

The Loire Valley boasts a rich tapestry of grape varieties, each contributing to its diverse and renowned wines. Sauvignon Blanc shines in Sancerre, while Chenin Blanc thrives in Vouvray. Cabernet Franc anchors the reds of Chinon, and Melon de Bourgogne stars in crisp Muscadet. These varieties epitomize the region's vinous excellence.

Sauvignon Blanc

Sauvignon Blanc, a noble white grape varietal, is a monument to winemaking expertise, and nowhere is this more evident than in the Loire Valley. Sauvignon Blanc has established a separate identity in the wine market due to its zesty acidity, aromatic character, and wide taste spectrum.

Sauvignon Blanc, which originated in the Bordeaux region of France, finds an excellent home in the

Loire Valley, where the cool climate and unique terroir add to the grape's lively character. Sauvignon Blanc from the Loire Valley is known for its crisp acidity, which gives the wines a refreshing flavor. This grape's expression varies from region to appellation, providing wine connoisseurs with a fascinating exploration.

Sauvignon Blanc reaches its greatest potential in the Loire Valley appellations of ==Sancerre== and ==Pouilly-Fumé.== These wines frequently have significant mineral notes as a result of the limestone-rich soils, which lend a particular flinty quality. Furthermore, the aromatic profile of the Loire Valley's Sauvignon Blanc is intriguing, with citrus fruits, green apple, and sometimes tropical undertones, making it a perfect companion for hot summer days.

Winemakers in the Loire Valley use a variety of winemaking procedures to enhance the natural characteristics of the grape. To preserve the grape's crisp acidity and the freshness of the fruit flavors, stainless steel fermentation and aging are widely used. Some producers, on the other hand, use oak aging to add subtle depth and texture to their wines.

Sauvignon Blanc from the Loire Valley is not only a sensory joy, but also a flexible meal partner. Its bright acidity complements a wide range of foods, from goat cheese salads to shellfish and chicken. Sauvignon Blanc, with its capacity to represent the region's particular terroir, is a monument to the region's winemaking tradition and current commitment to producing wines of high quality and character.

Chenin Blanc

Chenin Blanc, also known as the "queen of white grapes," is a versatile and highly regarded cultivar that has found its true home in France's Loire Valley. Chenin Blanc has successfully spanned the globe, leaving a great influence on the world of wine. Its origins may be traced back to the Anjou region.

Because of its resilience to varied climates and soil types, this grape is grown in a variety of wine areas, but its purest and most expressive varieties are unquestionably found in the Loire Valley. Chenin Blanc thrives in the chilly environment, limestone-rich soils, and various terroirs of this region, yielding wines ranging from bone-dry to lusciously sweet.

One of Chenin Blanc's distinctive characteristics is its remarkable acidity, which adds to its age-worthiness and capacity to make wines of tremendous complexity. Chenin Blanc exhibits a dazzling diversity of aromas in its dry expressions, featuring notes of green apple, quince, and honey, frequently complemented by a characteristic minerality. Because of the grape's sensitivity to noble rot, magnificent sweet wines, such as those from the Vouvray and Coteaux du Layon appellations, have emerged, demonstrating the grape's ability to make nectar-like elixirs with layers of apricot, lemon, and floral characteristics.

The attraction of Chenin Blanc extends beyond its flavor characteristics. Winemakers love its adaptability, which allows them to create a wide range of styles, from still and sparkling to dry and sweet. The grape's versatility gives it a perfect canvas for experimentation, resulting in wines that appeal to a wide range of tastes.

Chenin Blanc's prominence is increasing as buyers seek out unique and distinctive wines. Chenin Blanc continues to fascinate wine enthusiasts with its elegance, versatility, and ability to represent the character of the terroir in which it is grown, whether consumed in its birthplace in the Loire Valley or relished in new regions.

Cabernet Franc

Cabernet Franc, a red grape variety native to France's Bordeaux region, has won international renown for its distinct qualities and versatility in winemaking. While Cabernet Franc is frequently overshadowed by its more famous progeny, Cabernet Sauvignon, it is a unique variety with its own characteristics.

Cabernet Franc's potential to express terroir is one of its distinctive characteristics. The grape is especially sensitive to growing circumstances, adjusting to various soils and temperatures. Cabernet Franc creates wines with robust acidity, rich red fruit flavors, and flowery aromas in its native Loire Valley. These wines typically have a lighter body than Cabernet Sauvignon, making them approachable and food-friendly.

Cabernet Franc is an important component of the world-famous Bordeaux blend, where it adds elegance and aromatic depth. Cabernet Franc is essential in producing wines with elegance and a velvety texture in locations such as Saint-Émilion and Pomerol.

Cabernet Franc has achieved success outside of Bordeaux in a variety of regions across the world. Winemakers in the New World, particularly in California, Washington, and South America, have welcomed the grape and experimented with various types. Because of the grape's flexibility, wines ranging from light and flowery to strong and full-bodied have been produced, demonstrating its chameleon-like nature.

Cabernet Franc is known for its aromatic profile, which includes notes of raspberry, cherry, violet, and occasionally a trace of green bell pepper. The mild tannins and pleasant acidity of the grape lead to wines that are not only age-worthy but also appealing in their youth.

Cabernet Franc has recently earned a devoted following among wine connoisseurs who enjoy its diversity and representation of terroir. Cabernet Franc continues to enchant the palates of wine enthusiasts around the world, whether savored on its own or as part of a blend, proving that it deserves a place in the spotlight alongside its more recognized peers.

Melon de Bourgogne

Melon de Bourgogne, a white grape variety from Burgundy, found another home in France's westernmost vineyards, notably in the Pays Nantais region of the Loire Valley. This grape variety, often called Melon, rose to popularity in the creation of the region's famous crisp and minerally Muscadet wines.

Melon de Bourgogne was relocated due to historical events. After a severe frost destroyed Burgundy's vineyards in the 17th century, local winemakers sought a grape type more suited to the colder environment of the Loire Valley. They chose Melon de Bourgogne, a strong and durable vine that thrived in the Pays Nantais' marine climate. Muscadet, a wine that became synonymous with the region, was born as a result of this unexpected transfer.

Melon de Bourgogne grapes often create pale-colored wines with greenish tints. Muscadet wines are known for their strong acidity and invigorating freshness, making them perfect partners with seafood, particularly oysters from the adjacent Atlantic coast. The capacity of the grape to keep acidity even in cool climates contributes to the wine's durability and age-worthiness.

Melon de Bourgogne wines are distinguished by the terroir of the Loire Valley. The soils, which are predominantly formed of granite, schist, and gneiss, impart a noticeable minerality to the wines. The marine influence, with its temperature-moderating effect, boosts the grape's expression in the vines even more.

While Muscadet is the most common expression of Melon de Bourgogne, several winemakers in the region experiment with alternative winemaking techniques, such as barrel aging, to demonstrate the grape's adaptability. These efforts have yielded nuanced and varied expressions that highlight the grape's resilience and potential for creating wines of varying kinds within the Loire Valley's diverse viticultural terrain.

Gamay

Gamay is a red grape variety that has made a name for itself in France, particularly in the Beaujolais area and sections of the Loire Valley. Gamay produces wines that are approachable and food-friendly because of its sharp acidity, minimal tannins, and lively fruit notes.

Gamay has a primary home in Beaujolais, where it is the sole grape variety utilized in the manufacture of red wines. The most well-known expression of Gamay comes from the ten crus of Beaujolais, each with its own distinct terroir and characteristics. Beaujolais Nouveau, a young and fresh kind of wine released only a few weeks after harvest, has also acquired international acclaim, signaling the start of the annual wine celebration.

Gamay wines are known for their vibrant red fruit flavors, with notable notes of strawberry, raspberry, and occasionally cherry. The grape's gentle tannins make it highly drinkable, especially in its youth. Gamay wines are frequently light to medium-bodied, resulting in a refreshing and gulpable quality that is ideal for warm weather or as a versatile partner to a variety of foods.

Gamay is noted in the vineyard for its great yields and adaptability to varied soils. Its thin skin contributes to lower tannin levels and gives the wines a distinct brightness. Winemakers use a variety of vinification procedures, including carbonic maceration, to improve the finished product's fruity and flowery characteristics.

While Gamay has gained popularity in France, particularly in Beaujolais, it has also spread to other wine-producing regions across the world. Winemakers in Oregon and Canada are experimenting with this grape, making wines that highlight the distinct terroirs of their individual regions while remaining loyal to Gamay's intrinsic traits.

Gamay is a versatile and endearing grape variety that produces wines recognized for its fruity flavors, crisp acidity, and ease of drinking. Its ability to convey the nuances of many terroirs has led to its global popularity, making it an appealing choice for both wine connoisseurs and those new to the world of red wines.

Wine Regions

Anjou Region

In the western Loire Valley, Anjou is a wine area that surrounds the French city of Angers. It makes a variety of red, rosé, and white wines in still, sparkling, dry, and sweet styles.

The district's generic Anjou appellation produces unremarkable, unprestigious wines. However, there are a number of notable subregional AOPs inside the zone. Some examples are the sweet white nectars of Côteaux du Layon, the crisp Chenin Blanc of Savennières, and the aromatic Cabernet Franc of Saumur.

AOP Anjou

Red, white, and sparkling wines are all covered by the district-wide Anjou appellation; rosé wines are handled by the rosé-specific 'Rosé d'Anjou' and

'Cabernet d'Anjou' appellations. With a little assistance from Pineau d'Aunis and Gamay, Cabernet grapes are used mostly to make Anjou Rouge. Usually based on Chenin Blanc, Anjou Blanc frequently includes a small amount (up to 20 percent) of Chardonnay and Sauvignon Blanc.

Sparkling Anjou Mousseux is derived from the same range of grapes as the still wines and is available in both white and rosé versions. Red Anjou Gamay is the sole varietal wine produced under this appellation, and it has to be made entirely of Gamay. Like in Beaujolais, the spiritual birthplace of Gamay, these wines can be produced in the low-tannin, fruit-forward 'Primeur/Nouveau' style.

Additional AOPs in the Anjou Wine Area
Here in Anjou, sweet Chenin Blanc wines are a bit of a specialty. These are some of the most exquisite sweet wines produced in France; while they are not

as well-known as Sauternes, several of them are highly appreciated by connoisseurs.

The Côteaux du Layon zone produces the best of these, especially in the little sub-regions of Bonnezeaux and Quarts de Chaume. Their nose is honeyed and flowery, with notes of tropical fruit. Anjou-Côteaux de la Loire, or sweet wines from the immediate west of Angers, are among the district's lesser-known varieties.

Though Anjou's sweet wines are excellent with Chenin Blanc, the amount and quality of dry Chenin Blanc produced here are rising quickly. A little location directly west of Angers, Savennières (with its two sub-zones, Coulée de Serrant and La Roche aux Moines) produces some of the finest dry Chenin Blanc anywhere in the world.

Showcasing the diversity of the region, the dry, sweet white wines are paired with dry, slightly spicy red wines created from Cabernet Franc and bottled under the Anjou Villages label. The best of them are from the Brissac region's vineyards.

The rosé wines of Anjou are produced in two quite different ways. The market for the low-acid, semi-sweet Rosé d'Anjou is currently declining, despite its enormous popularity in the mid-to-late 20th century. Generally speaking, Cabernet d'Anjou is more complex, more structured, and finer.

In Saumur, a few sparkling rosés are produced. These primarily pair Chenin Blanc and/or Grolleau with Cabernet Franc.

Geographical Terroir The Loire River, which travels 620 miles (or a thousand kilometers) across the center of France, divides Anjou neatly in half. The Pays Nantais Muscadet vines are located to the west, and the Touraine district is located just upriver to the east. The geographic area of the district is almost equal to that of the former Duchy of Anjou. This is very similar to the administrative department of Maine-et-Loire today.

The continental impact of central France to the east and the coastal influence of the Atlantic to the west balance out the relatively temperate climate of Anjou. The Loire River adds a unique character to the area, resulting in somewhat different mesoclimates.

The soil types in the district can be broadly classified into two categories. The Armorican Massif's schist and carboniferous rocks are located to the north.

Soils rich in limestone and visibly whiter are more common in the west and south. The later soils are a clear indicator of Angers' placement on the Paris Basin's southern edge. It has something in common with Sancerre, the most well-known wine region in the Loire.

The Anjou grape area extends into the Pay Nantais to the west of Angers, intersecting with the Côteaux d'Ancenis and Muscadet titles, and ending only a little distance short of Nantes.

Subregions of Anjou

Anjou Villages

The Anjou district of the western Loire Valley wine region of France is best renowned for its sweet and dry white wines, but it also produces some superior red wines. These wines are referred to as Anjou Villages. It is far newer than many of its neighbors, having been implemented as of the 1991 harvest.

Less renowned regional varietals like Gamay and Grolleau Noir are not used in the production of Anjou Villages wines, which are only created from Cabernet Franc and Cabernet Sauvignon. They have scents of black cherries, red fruits, and a distinctive earthy spice note. They are very full-bodied, though not as full-bodied as their counterparts from Bordeaux and the south of France.

The Anjou Villages title was merely intended to serve as Anjou Rouge's more limited, regional counterpart. The appellation is limited to the best south-facing slopes in 46 communes, which includes the superior land parcels surrounding Anjou.

This generally corresponds to the region that the appellations Coteaux du Layon, Coteaux de la Loire, and Savennières cover. As a result, Chenin Blanc is not often grown in regions where red grapes are planted. Schist makes up the base of soils, and gravels can be added on top.

Anjou Villages wines are produced by over 120 wineries. The yearly production exceeds 940,000 bottles.

An additional subdivision was created in 1998 for the wines of Brissac (Brissac-Quince in its entirety) and the nine communes that are located within a three-mile radius of it. Anjou Villages-Brissac is the name given to these.

Bonnezeaux

The Anjou region in France's western Loire Valley is home to the renowned sweet white wine appellation Bonnezeaux. Only a small portion of the Thouarce commune, located approximately 15 kilometers (10 miles) south of Angers along the Loire river, is covered by the 1951 title.

Among the most esteemed sweet wines in the Loire, if not all of France, are Bonnezeaux wines. Pineau de la Loire, or Chenin Blanc, is the only ingredient used in their production. The name means "good waters" in translation.

The only Loire sweet wine known to be more renowned than Bonnezeaux is Quarts de Chaume, which is produced nine miles (or fourteen kilometers) to the northwest. This is explained by the Quarts de Chaume wines' renownedly limited vineyard location and their stricter production guidelines.

The Chaume Premier Cru Côteaux du Layon designation is another Chaume distinction that competes with Bonnezeaux. Despite being a sub-appellation of the easier-to-get-by Côteaux du Layon, Chaume shares Bonnezeaux's producing characteristics. In 2003, it was granted formal Premier Cru status.

Terroir

The vines used to make Bonnezeaux wine are situated in the sandy shale soils that make up the region's topography, covering about 90 hectares (220 acres). The Atlantic's oceanic effect moderates the climate in which they flourish. Their mesoclimate is moderately moist and dry, with above-average sunlight levels on the mild, south-facing slopes.

Bonnezeaux and the consecutive method's attempts

Harvesting of the grapes is done in multiple attempts. Throughout the course of several days and weeks, the vineyard is traversed several times, and only the ripest grapes impacted by the "noble" rot botrytis are harvested.

Jean Boivin, the winemaker widely recognized for having created the Bonnezeaux appellation in the first place, brought this technique to the Loire. He carried the method from his Sauternes harvests. It quickly gained popularity and extended to other regional names.

It is particularly symbolic that the technique should have come from Sauternes; just as the Loire, fed by the Layon and the Aubance, creates ideal conditions for the creation of botrytized wines, so the Garonne and its tributaries create a sinuous patchwork of meso climates in the southern Graves. Particularly for wines picked in this manner, the Selection de Grains Nobles label, which is currently found on a large number of Coteaux du Layon wines (imported from Alsace), is reserved.

Cabernet d'Anjou

The appellation Cabernet d'Anjou is devoted only to rosé Anjou wines produced from the 'Cabernet' grapes, which are a blend of Cabernet Sauvignon and Cabernet Franc. Cabernet Franc's signature scents, which include strawberry, raspberry, and roses, are found in Cabernet d'Anjou wines, which are fruit-driven and more complex than ordinary rosé wines. There is also a hint of white pepper towards the finish.

Often, the wines are slightly sugary or even off-dry. They are more commercially available now than their Rosé d'Anjou counterparts, but they are also more ageworthy due to their well-balanced acidity and strong tannic structure.

Anjou Gamay is another varietal appellation for the Anjou section of the western Loire Valley. This only holds true for red wines.

The 150 communes that make up the district, which stretches from Saumur in the east to Champtoceaux in the west, are the source of a Cabernet d'Anjou wine. This region represents the border between the whiter, limestone-rich soils of the southern Paris Basin and the carboniferous soils of the Armorican Massif.

'Primeur' or 'Nouveau' labels may be applied to Cabernet d'Anjou wines. Both names describe a considerably fruitier type of wine that is fermented using carbonic maceration, which almost eliminates tannins. Such wines cannot be released before the 38th day leading up to the third Thursday of November in the harvest year, according to official appellation regulations.

Cabernet de Saumur

The sole rosé-specific appellation in Saumur, a town and district in the central Loire Valley wine region of France, is Cabernet de Saumur. The title was created in 1964 and has a low annual production of 460,000 liters.

Any Cabernet de Saumur wine must contain at least 85% Cabernet Franc. An optional (15 percent) addition of Cabernet Sauvignon or Pineau d'Aunis might be used to balance this.

Light-bodied and relatively high in acidity, a typical Cabernet de Saumur wine is a key component of its fruit-forward, crisp, refreshing taste. While Cabernet de Saumur wines are usually less sweet than their Cabernet d'Anjou cousins, they can nonetheless have up to 10 grams of residual sugar per liter.

With the exception of very hot vintages like 2003, this sweetness is nearly always counterbalanced by natural acidity, which is a product of the cold environment here in the central Loire. The wines are best enjoyed within two years after vintage, almost without exception.

Cabernet de Saumur wines can range from very dry to semi-sweet, and they can also be marketed as Nouveau (like Beaujolais Nouveau, which is a more well-known example), which means that they are released shortly after harvest.

Coteaux de l'Aubance

The Anjou region in the western Loire Valley of France is home to the sweet wine appellation Coteaux de l'Aubance. The local terroir is ideal for Chenin Blanc grapes, which are used alone to make these wines. The most popular variety in the Loire for sweet wines is chenin, or Pineau de la Loire as it is called locally.

It was first implemented in 1950 and encompasses ten communes south of Angers. About 40 producers are connected to the AOP. All of the A produce about 800,000 bottles a year.

All of the wines, meanwhile, aren't thought to be among the greatest examples of the Loire. Coteaux du Layon, its neighbor to the south, has long enjoyed greater esteem and recognition.

Rather than any superiority of terroir, this is due to the historical caliber of winemaking in the respective appellations. Currently, things are beginning to change as more renowned winemakers are creating Coteaux de l'Aubance that is of a higher caliber.

The topography of southern Anjou, which was mostly formed by the Aubance and other regional river systems, is largely responsible for the high caliber of its sweet wines. The Aubance has sculpted gentle, south-facing slopes and isolated meso climates over millennia, shielding the vineyards from frigid continental winds that come from the north and east.

The river leaves gravel-rich banks on its previous path in the village of Brissac-Quince, when it bends west from its northerly course. Vine from Coteaux de l'Aubance is grown here, in the schistous soils that sit between the Aubance and the Loire. There are also signs of slate in the soils.

The Aubance river's early mists in late summer encourage the growth of botrytis, a crucial component of the most expressive Coteaux de l'Aubance wines. The sweetest of them are offered for sale as Noble Grains Coteaux de l'Aubance Sélection.

Anjou Villages-Brissac, which is based on Cabernet Franc, is also produced in this region. Some of Anjou's best red wines are produced under this appellation.

Coteaux de Saumur

The only sweet, late-harvest wine designation in Saumur, located in the French Loire Valley wine area, is Coteaux de Saumur. Since its creation in 1962, the appellation has produced a very little amount of wine each year, especially when compared to the sweet white experts located directly to the west (such as those of the Coteaux du Layon).

The rules for producing both wines are similar, even if they differ in terms of production volume and general recognition. Both come only from Chenin Blanc and are harvested with a minimum sugar concentration of 238g/L (the latter requirement only applies to Coteaux du Layon labels that specify a specific commune; the minimum sugar level for regular Coteaux du Layon is 221g/L).

In reality, pickers gather just the ripest grapes and, when applicable, those impacted by botrytis throughout numerous passes through the vineyard to harvest both wines in "tries successives."

Just six communes on the Loire River, southwest and south of Saumur, are included in the term. As a result, only about 40,000 liters (10,500 US gallons) of wine are produced each year. This is a small amount of the 4.5 million liters (1.2 million US gallons) produced under the Coteaux du Layon sweet wine appellation overall, and far less than the single Layon village of Chaume.

Because of this, Coteaux de Saumur wines are typically pricey and uncommon outside of France, where they are sold almost exclusively to end users.

Like the rest of the Saumur district, the vineyards' soils are loose and gravelly near the Loire River's banks and rich in "tuffeau" soils higher up. Tuffeau is a delicate, yellowish sedimentary rock that is unique to the Loire region. It developed about 90 million years ago during the Turonian age, which was called after Touraine.

The incredibly porous rock, which is a mixture of sand and marine fossils, absorbs water quickly and releases it gradually. These characteristics make them perfect for viticulture because they keep reserves that prevent the plants from completely shutting down during dry spells and drain surplus water from the roots of the vines.

Coteaux du Layon

The greatest appellation for sweet wines in the Anjou section of the Loire Valley is Coteaux du Layon. It was first implemented in 1950 and spans 27 communes south of Angers, with 1,700 hectares (4,200 acres) of grapes under its jurisdiction.

The only grape used to make Coteaux du Layon wines is Chenin Blanc, which grows well in the region's schistous soils. The most popular variety in the Loire for sweet wines is chenin, or Pineau de la Loire as it is known locally. It peaks in the catchment area of the Coteaux du Layon and Coteaux de l'Aubance, which are to the north.

Particularly good sweet wines are known to come from a select few of these communes. They have thereby gained the ability to include their village names as a component of the appellation title, or their own independent appellations.

Quarts de Chaume and Bonnezeaux (a little community near to Faye d'Anjou) are two that have their own names. The former only includes a tiny portion of Rochefort-sur-Loire.

Beaulieu-sur-Layon, Faye d'Anjou, Rochefort-sur-Loire, Saint-Lambert-du-Lattay, Rablay-sur-Layon, and Saint-Aubin-de-Luigne are the "Villages" level designations. The "Pearl of the Layon" is the title given to the latter. Links to the pertinent region pages can be found in the menu on the left.

The geography of the region, which is a product of the nearby river systems, especially the Layon, is largely responsible for the superior quality of the region's sweet wines. The river has sculpted pockets of protected meso climates and gentle, south-facing slopes over millennia, shielding the vineyards from the chilly continental winds that come from the north and east.

The morning mists originating from the river encourage the growth of botrytis in late summer. The greatest wines from Coteaux du Layon must include this component.

The designation Selection de Grains Nobles appears after the appellation name on the sweetest Coteaux du Layon wines. They are created by picking only grapes that have noble rot, which is gathered during several passes through the vineyard.

Quarts de Chaume Grand Cru appellation

The Quarts de Chaume Grand Cru appellation, located in the Anjou section of the western Loire Valley of France, is a highly esteemed sweet white wine. Chenin Blanc, sometimes referred to as Pineau de la Loire, is the only grape used to make Quarts de Chaume wines.

Established in 1954, the appellation has grown to become one of the most well-known brands in the Loire and is regarded as one of the most coveted names in France's selection of dessert wines. In this sense, Bonnezeaux, which is 13 kilometers/8 miles to the southeast, is comparable. Still, neither has quite achieved the renown of the crisp, dry whites of Pouilly-Fumé and Sancerre.

Situated a mere 40 hectares (100 acres) of vineyards, the Quarts de Chaume label is one of the most location-specific appellations in the Loire.

These are located in the Rochefort-sur-Loire parish near the southern end of Chaume, a hamlet.

The lieux-dits of Les Rousses, Le Veau, and Les Quarts are corresponding to this area. Slopes that face south are ideal for vine placement. The complicated geology includes pudding stones and schist.

About twenty wineries produce wines under this appellation. An average of 40,000 liters (or 53,000 bottles) are produced annually.

The only marginally less prestigious Coteaux du Layon Chaume encompasses the remainder of Chaume. To make things even more confusing, Coteaux du Layon Rochefort-sur-Loire, a third appellation for sweet white wines, encompasses the entire commune of Rochefort-sur-Loire. In terms of reputation, this is a rung down on the ladder.

Chaume vs Chaume Quarts

Concerning the years, there has been some debate concerning Chaume's three sweet wine appellations and overall production of excellent sweet wines. The wineries who have been fortunate enough to have their wines awarded the Quarts de Chaume title have fiercely guarded the distinction and exclusivity of this label.

The committee for the Quarts de Chaume appellation pushed to have the 2003 upgrade of the Coteaux du Layon Chaume désignation to Chaume Premier Cru des Coteaux du Layon reversed. They said that since the new Premier Cru would be the first the Loire had ever seen, it would lead to misunderstanding with their own moniker and give them an unfair advantage.

Thereafter, there was a brief suspension of the Premier Cru Chaume title. In 2009, Quarts de

Chaume was granted Grand Cru designation (effective 2014), thus reinstating its status.

Rosé d'Anjou

The appellation Rosé d'Anjou is used to identify rosé wines from the Anjou district in the western Loire Valley wine region of France. Traditionally linked to more fruity rosés produced primarily from Grolleau Noir, the designation is currently losing significance. This is especially true when contrasting it with the more serious and sophisticated rosé wines produced under the Cabernet d'Anjou label.

A varietal that is allowed under relatively few other appellations is Grolleau Noir. Although fewer vines are being planted, those that haven't been replaced by more commercially successful cultivars— Cabernet Franc is a prime example—end up in Rosé d'Anjou. These wines may now also contain Cabernet Franc, Cabernet Sauvignon, Malbec (called locally as Cot), Gamay, Pineau d'Aunis, and Grolleau Gris in an effort to improve their quality and popularity.

The 150 communes that make up the district, which stretches from Saumur in the east to Champtoceaux in the west, are the source of a Rosé d'Anjou wine. This region represents the border between the whiter, limestone-rich soils of the southern Paris Basin and the carboniferous soils of the Armorican Massif.

'Primeur' or 'Nouveau' labels may be applied to Rosé d'Anjou wines. The carbonic maceration method of fermentation results in a considerably fruitier wine that is nearly free of tannins. According to official legislation, the wines cannot be made public before the 38th day leading up to the third Thursday of November in the harvest year in order for this title to be valid.

Saumur

In the center of France's Loire Valley sits the mid-sized town and wine appellation of Saumur. The designation applies to sparkling white and rosé wines as well as still white, rosé, and red wines. Saumur's dry reds are the most sought-after wines in the early twenty-first century, however the region produces a sizable amount of sparkling wines, which stole the show in the second half of the 20th century.

Saumur region

The production region of still wines is centered on Saumur (in the Maine-et-Loire department), primarily on the southern bank of the Loire. It extends outward from the town center of Saumur for about 30 km (18 miles), into the adjacent administrative departments of Vienne and Deux-Sèvres.

Although, in general, they are relatively contiguous, the zones for white, rosé, and red production do not overlap altogether. A somewhat larger area, around 40 km (25 miles) west of Saumur town, is included in the production of sparkling wine.

The Saumur Puy-Notre-Dame title, which encompasses three separate localities just southwest and southeast of Saumur town, is a final sub regional designation (technically a "geographically complementary denomination"). All of Saumur Puy-Notre-Dame's wines are red.

Grape varietals

While Saumur rosé can be made from Cabernet Franc and/or Cabernet Sauvignon, Saumur blanc (white) is exclusively based around the region's mainstay Chenin Blanc, sometimes also referred to as Pineau de la Loire.

Although Pineau d'Aunis and Cabernet Sauvignon may appear in trace amounts—no more than 30% of any blend—Cabernet Franc is also the main ingredient in Saumur rouge (red wine). Moreover, Cabernet Franc makes up the majority of Saumur Puy-Notre-Dame, with up to 15% going to Cabernet Sauvignon.

According to general criteria, the majority of sparkling wines, whether white or rosé, should be Chenin Blanc (for Saumur mousse blanc/white) or Cabernet Franc (for Saumur mousseux rosé). These types must comprise at least 60% of the variety in each category.

Several regional and international varietals, including as Chardonnay, Sauvignon Blanc, Cabernet Sauvignon, Gamay, Grolleau Gris, Grolleau, Pineau d'Aunis, and Pinot Noir, can make up the last 40% or less of a sparkling blend. The sole restriction is that the percentage of Sauvignon Blanc in any sparkling wine cannot exceed 10%.

Rouge Saumur

The region is currently better recognized for its classic Saumur rouge (red), which has earthy, peppery, herbal notes and a trace of pencil shavings. It boasts fruity, flowery scents of violets and slightly under ripe plums. Because Cabernet Franc makes up a substantial portion of their composition, they are typically prepared with pronounced tannins even though they are rather light-bodied.

Situated only a few kilometers east of Chinon and Bourgueil, these lively, aromatic, and crisp wines share a lot of stylistic similarities. Loire Valley's best and most respected red wines come from this group of red wine appellations.

It is important to distinguish the wines of Saumur-Champigny from those in the larger Saumur group. Established as a classification for the greatest wines created in the greater Saumur region, this particular appellation is based on eight villages close to the city of Saumur. Although the wines are regarded as an improvement over Saumur rouge, they are nevertheless based on Cabernet Franc and have the same supporting varietals as Saumur.

Although the local red wines are currently gaining popularity, Saumur's sparkling wines remain the district's most important product in terms of quantity. Many long-standing firms, the most well-known of which are Bouvet-Ladubay and Gratien & Meyer, manufacture large quantities of excellent value Saumur Mousseux every year. The Taittinger Group currently owns the former, which opened its doors in 1851. Henkell, the behemoth of German sparkling wine, currently owns the latter, which was started in 1864 by Alfred Gratien of the Champagne house bearing his name.

Saumur's topography

Sparkling wine production is especially well adapted to Saumur's geology. Perched atop a pile of porous, sandy-yellow granite known as tuffeau, the village overlooks many of the best vineyard sites in the middle Loire. Deep underground, miles of cellars have been carved out of this soft rock, offering a cool, temperate environment ideal for aging méthode traditionelle wines on their lees.

The region produces very little wine other than white and rosé each year in Saumur. These have historically had a somewhat bland flavor and character, being heavily cropped and produced as a backup option for sparkling wine.

But there have been sporadic improvements in quality due to the present surge in demand for high-grade Chenin Blanc. With the same boundaries as Saumur AOC, the Cabernet de Saumur appellation for rosé wines is only applicable to off-dry wines with a minimum of 10 grams of residual sugar per liter.

The small amount of sweet wine produced in the Saumur region is marketed under the Côteaux de Saumur designation. In terms of quantity, it produces very little, and in terms of quality, it is not as good as the highly esteemed sweet wines made in the Côteaux du Layon zone, to the west.

Saumur-Champigny

The main ingredient of Saumur-Champigny wines is Cabernet Franc, although up to 15% of Cabernet Sauvignon and/or Pineau d'Aunis (also referred to as "Chenin Noir") may be added, albeit this is rarely done. The wines have upfront, slightly spicy, berry fruit notes and sharp acidity; they are usually light to medium-bodied.

The area used for vineyards

Currently, each vintage of Saumur-Champigny red wine produces about 7.4 million liters. The vineyard, which spans over 1,500 hectares (3,700 acres) and is situated within the Saumur and Souzay-Champigny parishes, together with six other neighbors, is the source of the grapes. This essentially travels seven kilometers (four miles) north to south and fifteen kilometers (9 miles) along the Loire River's southern bank, connecting Saumur to the west and Montsoreau to the east.

The southernmost commune, Saint-Cyr-en-Bourg, is home to some of the most important vineyards that produce Saumur-Champigny wine. In actuality, the village's wine cooperative was a major force behind the cultivation of Cabernet Franc in the region and contributed significantly to the creation of this appellation.

Terroir Champigny was designated as a distinct appellation because of its exceptional terroir, which is essential to the creation of wines in this style. At the eastern side of Saumur town, a low plateau of tuffeau, the yellowish metamorphic rock that is so characteristic of the central Loire region, rises. It stretches virtually continuously for seven miles (11 km) to the settlement of Candes Saint-Martin, which is located immediately east of Montsoreau.

Much of the taste of Saumur wine comes from this sandy, porous rock, which instantly absorbs excess water and stores it for use during the driest times of the year to control the vines' water supply. Dry, free-draining soils are beneficial to vines, and they seldom experience excessive water stress while growing in tuffeau-rich soils.

A modest marine impact from the Atlantic Ocean moderates the climate of Saumur, although it is lessened by the 160 km (100 miles) of low-lying fields and woodland that stand between it. Still, the Loire's sluggish currents offer little relief from the summer's heat. The summertime heat is said to have inspired Champigny's original Latin name, Campus Ignis ("Field of Fire"), according to local legend.

History

This site-specific title was established in December 1957 as an addition to the Saumur Rouge appellation, which was also established at the same time and under the same decree. The wines saw a significant fashion shift within ten vintages of the title's introduction, a trend that persisted until the 1990s.

This was particularly true for the elites of Paris, for whom the Loire Valley has long served as a weekend getaway. It is common to refer to the area between Angers and Orleans in particular as the "playground" of the French nobles.

Due to its increasing popularity, Saumur-Champigny's wine output had a significant growth, resulting in the vineyards' surface area doubling and tripling. Many vignerons started emphasizing both quality and quantity in their wine production during this period, and they have helped to maintain Saumur-Champigny's positive reputation far into the new millennium.

The Saumur Puy-Notre Dame appellation, which encompasses a little bigger territory just south and west of the Saumur-Champigny catchment area, was formally introduced in October 2009. What impact this will have on Saumur-Champigny's wines, domaines, and reputation is still unknown.

Savennières

The Loire Valley in France is home to the renowned white wine appellation of Savennières. Situated in the larger Anjou district, the parish bearing the same name is just southwest of the city of Angers. The primary grape of Anjou and the central Loire, Chenin Blanc, is used to make the wines.

Although sweeter varieties are allowed, dry white wines are most commonly associated with this appellation. They are considered to be among the best in the whole Loire region. They are the Vouvray and Sancerre of the western Loire region, in terms of quality.

Warm straw, beeswax, and chamomile are among the strong characteristics that characterize most savennières wines. The finest have a noticeable minerality, and the ripest even have a hint of honey. Once defining all of Savennieres' production, botrytis is now less prevalent in the wines produced there.

The low maximum yield constraints imposed by appellation legislation result in very concentrated wines that have a surprisingly lengthy shelf life. In their youth, many consumers perceive the most structured wines to be excessively acidic and steely; they are similar to excellent Chablis. Approximately five years in the bottle causes this character to start to fade.

Savennières wine has been sweet, or at least off-dry, for the most of its existence. Both producers and customers started gravitating toward the drier style that we are familiar with in the later decades of the 20th century. In Anjou's sea of sweet wine, Savennières now proudly stands alone as the only appellation for dry white wine.

Generally speaking, vines thrive on Loire river bank slopes with good ventilation. The sandstone schist foundation of the shallow soils is interspersed with sand and volcanic rock seams.

Just to the west are the vineyards that produce the Coteaux de la Loire wines of Anjou. The Coteaux du Layon and Coteaux de l'Aubance appellations are located to the south and east, respectively, across the Loire. These regions produce some dry wines. But there aren't as many of them, and the wines don't get as much attention abroad.

The original appellation laws from 1952 were amended in 1996 to include clarifications about the wines' levels of sweetness. It is now official that standard Savennières (without any sign of sweetness) is a dry wine. Higher levels of residual sugar are indicated by the Demi-sec and Moelleux and Doux declarations. Maximum yield constraints of 4,000 liters per hectare, instead of the usual 5,000, apply to these sweeter wines.

The Savennières appellation is divided into two crus, or named vineyard areas: Coulée de Serrant and La Roche aux Moines. The former is owned exclusively by Nicolas Joly, a pioneering producer. He is among the few producers working in the latter.

About thirty companies manufacture wines from Savennières. An average of 533,000 bottles are produced annually.

Auvergne Region

Southern central France contains the administrative area of Auvergne. The Massif Central's modest mountains and slopes dominate it.

These central French vineyards are known for producing light-bodied reds, or rosés, from Gamay that are vinified using carbonic maceration. This style is unique to Côte Roannaise and Côtes du Forez, and it was popularized by Beaujolais, which is located close east. The whites are primarily made from Chardonnay, however some are also produced from Sacy (Tresallier), primarily in Saint-Pourcain.

Auvergne's predominant feature is its varied topography and varied landscape, which directly influences the regional wine styles. The majority of Auvergne vineyards are located between 400 and 500 meters (1,300 and 1,650 feet) above sea level, and the region's continental climate results in considerably colder average yearly temperatures than those of neighboring Burgundy and the Rhône Valley. Wines with less thick structure result from this.

The temperature and a shorter growing season are suitable for grape varieties that ripen earlier. Their pleasant acidity and fruity fragrances are what they rely on.

Numerous rivers rise among these hills' summits; the Allier and the Loire are the two most significant (at least in terms of wine). The most common association of the first name is with oak barrels (the world's best originate from the old Allier oak forests). France's longest river, the Loire, is located in a major wine region of the nation.

Both of these rivers have sculpted out valleys, lakes, and alluvial plains along their routes through the Massif Central over millions of years as they make their way towards the lower-lying regions of northern and western France. Eventually, they come together in the very center of France, some 25 miles (40 km) south of Sancerre. The powerful Loire continues northward from this point and becomes the core of the Loire Valley wine area, which turns west.

Traditional vine-growing regions border both the Allier and the higher reaches of the Loire. At least since the Roman era, wine has been produced here, and several traditional varieties are still in use today. Even with this lengthy past, not many wines from this region have ever been well-known. Their light structure and lack of ageing potential may be the cause of this, although the isolated location may also have an impact.

For example, Saint-Pourcain is located 110 km (70 miles) from the closest notable appellations,

Pouilly-Fumé to the north and Pouilly-Fuissé to the east, which are sometimes mistaken. It seems to make sense that wine regions close to ports or important trade routes—like Bordeaux—have seen greater commercial success than those without a reliable export route.

Subregions of Auvergne

Châteaumeillant

A little region of the Centre-Loire produces red and rosé wines under the Châteaumeillant appellation in France. With some Pinot Noir, Gamay is the primary varietal used to produce the wines. Pinot Gris could also be a part of the rosés.

Vin gris, or extremely pale pink wines, have historically been linked to the Chateaumeillant moniker. The Gamay grapes used to make these are gently crushed. But red wine makes up 70:30 of the total yield.

The town that gives the appellation, which is situated between Bourges, Saint-Pourçain, and Poitou, is surrounded by seven parishes. The town in question is the closest to both Quincy and Menetou-Salon.

There are about 222 acres, or 90 hectares, of vineyards overall. The entire yearly production is about 420,000 liters. 300,000 of which is wine, red wine.

The coolest vineyard in the Centre-Loire is Châteaumeillant, which is situated in the Massif Centrale foothills. Its climate is continental, with chilly winters and hot summers. Rainfall averages 800 mm (32 in) every year. Sandstone, schist, and gneiss metamorphic subsoils are covered with sandy and silty clay silica soils.

Because of the appellation's small production and unproven reputation, wines from Chateaumeillant are extremely uncommon outside of France. 'On n'achète pas... Châteaumeillant, sauf si l'on est du coin,' said a local producer, meaning that one doesn't purchase Chateaumeillant unless they live nearby.

Since the fifth century, vines have been planted here. But AOC status would not materialize until 2010.

Côtes d'Auvergne

The appellation Cotes d'Auvergne has 53 parishes that are roughly 80 km (50 miles) long and 15 km (9 miles) wide. It passes across the middle of the Puy-de-Dome administrative department in central France. Since the appellation centers around the Allier River, a tributary of the Loire, it is typically categorized as a part of the Loire Valley. Though physically closer to the Rhone Valley and southern Burgundy, it is officially a part of the Auvergne region.

Just to the north, at the same time as Saint-Pourcain, the Cotes d'Auvergne title was first established in 1951 as a VDQS. It was classified at that level until 2012, when the INAO elevated it to full AOC status in response to a successful appeal by the regional winegrowers' union.

Currently, about 860 acres, or 350 hectares, are planted to vines. These are often distributed throughout the growing region in little vineyard parcels, or parcelles. With about 50 independent producers and one cooperative (which is serviced by about 100 growers), viticulture is primarily a family-run business.

Seventy-five percent of the region's wine production is made up of red wines. Although Pinot Noir, which accounts for 20% of vines, is also allowed, Gamay, the primary variety that makes up 50% of all vineyard acreage, will typically be used to produce these wines. Within the appellation, rosé wines are also produced.

The sole other officially recognized variety inside the appellation is Chardonnay, intended for use in the manufacture of white wine. Currently, vines are grown on about 350 hectares (860 acres) in total.

Although the terroir varies greatly throughout the appellation, it is typically impacted by the prehistoric volcanic activity of the Massif Central. However, examining the five sub-regional names that may be found on the label in addition to the "Cotes d'Auvergne" designation is the best way to characterize the diverse climates. From north to south, these are:

- Madrague is a red wine wine title situated on a tiny hill of white marl. It is centered on the village of Riom, about 10 kilometers (6 miles) north of Clermont-Ferrand.

- Just south of Madrague is the red wine subregion known as Châteaugay, which stretches along the edge of an old basaltic lava flow that has since fragmented into several smaller plateaux.

- The Chanturgue region, which is centered in Clermont-Ferrand, the department's capital, and partially overlaps with Châteaugay's vineyards, is known for its steep, volcanic basalt plateau vineyards.

- South of Clermont-Ferrand, the Corent sub-region is the only one dedicated to rosé wine. Here, grapes are concentrated around the hillsides of an ancient volcano, or "puy," with black soils and colluvial volcanic stone.

- The three communes that comprise Boudes, the southernmost part of the appellation, are remote and situated about 15 km south of the other Cotes d'Auvergne communes. This sub-region, known for its red wine, has vineyards scattered across a sizable limestone hill that is topped with basalt lava.

Châteaugay, with 65 hectares (160 acres) planted to vines, is by far the largest title. But the most well-liked are Corent and Boudes.

The area is thought to have a semi-continental climate. There is about 600 mm of rainfall a year, and the summers are hot and dry.

The central French plateau's volcanic, occasionally hilly terrain generates a "foehn" wind, a warm, dry wind that occurs on the leeside of mountains, which frequently tempers the typically damp westerly winds.

Although the history of viticulture in the area is probably much older, it was first documented in the fifth century. Throughout the Middle Ages, grape growing persisted. After the French Revolution, smallholding expansion led to a noticeable increase in the amount of land used for vine cultivation, reaching 34,000 hectares (84,000 acres) by 1850.

By the beginning of the 19th century, the grape area had grown to 45,000 hectares (111,000 acres) before Phylloxera's ravages. Despite efforts to restore the area in the early decades of the 20th century, this significantly declined.

Nowadays, consumers in mainland France and several western European nations purchase the majority of the reasonably priced Cotes d'Auvergne wines.

The region's vineyards also produce Pinot Noir and Chardonnay, among other varietals besides Gamay. These comprise wines from varietals such as Viognier, Sauvignon Blanc, and Petite Sirah (Durif), albeit they would need to be labeled under the more inclusive IGP Puy-de-Dome or Vin de France designations.

Saint-Pourçain

The appellation Saint-Pourçain is used to identify white, red, and rosé wines from 19 communes surrounding Saint-Pourçain-sur-Sioule, a small town in the Auvergne region of central France, in that order of significance. In December 1951, the appellation was first established as a VDQS, and in October 2009, it was elevated to full AOC rank.

The light skinned Sacy grape variety, sometimes known as Tressallier here, is the traditional variety used to make white Saint-Pourçain wines. But according to the appellation standards of today, the predominant varietal must be the more well recognized Chardonnay, with Tressallier and an optional 10 percent Sauvignon following.

Tressallier's fragrant, slightly spicy flavor profile sometimes draws comparisons to Viognier. That's why whites from Saint-Pourcain have a very distinct flavor.

The AOC produces red wines as well as white wines, albeit its white wines are its specialty. The predominant red variety in the chilly, steep Auvergne area is Gamay, which is required to make up at least 40% of all Saint-Pourçain red and/or rosé wines. Accompanying it is Pinot Noir, which has been aged in oak for a while (up to 60 percent at this point).

Nowadays, 1,480 acres (just over 600 hectares) of vines are planted for Saint-Pourçain wines. Over the previous ten years, this number has gradually climbed, especially once the name was given full AOC status. France and western Europe are the primary consumers of the more than 3.2 million liters of wine produced annually by the vineyards.

Crémant de Loire Region

The heartland of France's Loire Valley wine area, Anjou, Saumur, and Touraine, produce sparkling wines known by the appellation Crémant de Loire. The main component is Chenin Blanc.

Numerous more conventional Loire grape varieties can be employed. The conventional Chardonnay and Pinot Noir selections are among them, but there's also Cabernet Franc, Pineau d'Aunis, Grolleau Noir, and even Cabernet Sauvignon.

A noticeable (and deliberate) omission here is Sauvignon Blanc, the premier crop of the upper Loire. Loire Sauvignon is not regarded as being well adapted to the manufacture of sparkling wine, despite its strong acidity. It's interesting to note, though, that Bordeaux sparkling wines do contain this type.

An excellent Crémant de Loire has a nose that is complex, nutty, and lightly honeyed, and it has a tight, persistent effervescence that indicates méthode traditionnelle rather than tank production. These wines have more flowery scents than Champagne since Chenin Blanc is used in them. These are particularly noticeable in wines that have been left on the lees for a long time—the majority of Crémant is fermented in bottles for at least nine months.

The name was first used in 1975 to give France a well-known, premium Loire sparkling wine brand and a dependable substitute for the progressively more costly Champagne wines. Around the same period, its equivalents, Crémant de Bourgogne and Crémant d'Alsace, were introduced.

Every year, more than 14 million liters of Crémant de Loire are made. About 10% of the production is rosé, and the great bulk is white.

Vine covering around 1,500 hectares (3,700 acres) is dispersed throughout the appellation's catchment region. The center of the Loire's sparkling wine industry, Saumur, is actually where most of the wines are vinified.

Pays Nantais Region

The Pays Nantais region is well-known for its crisp, light white wines, some of which have been matured in lees.

The region surrounding Nantes on the Atlantic coast of west France, where the Loire river empties into the sea, is known as the Pays Nantais, or literally, "the land of Nantes". Between the coast of the Bay of Biscay in the west and adjacent Anjou in the east, the territory spans around 90 kilometers (55 miles) from east to west. It is located near the westernmost point of the larger Loire wine area as a result.

Wine varieties and styles

The majority of output produces crisp, light white wine varieties. Without a doubt, the most well-known of them is Muscadet, whose Melon de Bourgogne grape variety predominates in plantings throughout the area. In turn, various appellations are used to produce mussac wines, with the most common being Muscadet Sèvre-et-Maine.

Since melon de Bourgogne is not a particularly flavorful variety, the wines could end up being rather bland and featureless if proper care is not taken in the vineyard and throughout the winemaking process. This is especially true in hotter vintages, when the grapes tend to lose their distinctive, lively acidity as well as their organoleptic complexity.

Many wines are kept "sur lie"—that is, on the fine lees left over from alcoholic, or primary fermentation—for weeks or even months in order to extract as much flavor and character as possible from the grape must. Once more, Muscadet Sèvre-et-Maine produces some of the best Sur Lie wines.

Additional grape varieties

In the Pays Nantais, other grape types are planted for red wines such as Gamay, Cabernet Franc, and Cabernet Sauvignon, and for white wines, Chenin Blanc and Pinot Gris. You can use any of these for the Coteaux d'Ancenis appellation wines.

This region is also noted for its cultivation of Folle Blanche, sometimes referred to locally as "Gros Plant," which gave rise to the moniker Gros Plant du Pays Nantais.

Subregions of Pays Nantais

Coteaux d'Ancenis

In the western Loire Valley, midway between Nantes and Angers, sits the little wine region known as Coteaux d'Ancenis. The wines could be white, rosé, or red.

Gamay is the primary grape used to make reds and rosés, while up to 10% Cabernet Franc is permitted. For the white wines, only Pinot Gris is permitted.

Additionally, the area is noted for producing a sweet, late harvest Pinot Gris that is called "Malvoisie" locally and is frequently labeled as such (western Swiss wine producers, namely Vaud and Valais, use a similar naming scheme).

As a result, Coteaux d'Ancenis' wine selection is a little more varied than that of Muscadet and Gros Plant du Pays Nantais, two nearby appellations.

Both of them have a single approved grape variety and solely make white wines.

Coteaux d'Ancenis wines are frequently labeled as monovarietal, even though the reds do include some Cabernet Franc. As previously mentioned, the term "Malvoisie" typically indicates a wine with a significantly greater residual sugar content (approximately between 15 and 30 grams per liter, though this will vary greatly from producer to producer). The "Pinot Gris" label is frequently used to signify dry to off-dry white wines.

While Malvoisie isn't as good as the more renowned Bonnezeaux or Quarts de Chaume from the Loire, it can still be competitive in regional markets. Despite being somewhat of a local icon, Malvoisie is still produced in limited quantities.

Rosé and light-colored reds make up the majority of the wines (approximately 80% of production); light-colored reds make up nearly half of the production. Given that Gamay is used to make them, they may resemble Beaujolais and Beaujolais Nouveau in terms of style.

To the east of Nantes, along the Loire River, the vineyard region extends all the way to the western boundaries of Anjou. This region, which forms the eastern boundary of the Pays Nantais, has particularly metamorphic soils; on the north bank of the Loire, schist predominates, while on the south bank, gneiss and green schist coexist.

About 160 hectares (395 acres) of vines are grown, mostly in 27 communes in the departments of Maine-et-Loire and Loire-Atlantique.

With less rainfall than the majority of the Pays Nantais, the climate is characterized as temperate oceanic.

Muscadet

Muscadet, once associated with over-cropped, bland dry wines, is seeing a bit of a comeback, going back to its roots as a crisp white wine with varied degrees of complexity that pairs well with shellfish.

The main designation for the Pays Nantais, which is the area of the western Loire Valley surrounding Nantes on the country's central west coast, is mussac. The term refers only to white wines produced from Melon de Bourgogne, sometimes known as just Melon, which was also known as Muscadet in the past.

Sometimes confusion arises from the name Muscadet being similar to the Muscat grape family, but one sip of a crisp, dry Muscadet wine will prove beyond a shadow of a doubt that it is not produced from Muscat grapes.

With a production higher than nearly all other single wines in France (red Bordeaux comes in first), mussac has long been the go-to wine when pairing shellfish. Nobility from Paris used to vacation in the Loire Valley, where they constructed the chateaux that today dot the bucolic scenery.

Images of platters of fruits de mer and chilled glasses of Muscadet continue to make it a favorite domestic tourist destination in modern France. In the 1970s and 80s, the wines gained a lot of popularity in the United Kingdom, but they met the same end as the mass-produced German Riesling that was also well-liked at the time. In both instances, manufacturers favored quantity over quality due to the wines' explosive popularity, which ultimately caused the brands to lose value.

Cotes de Grandlieu, Coteaux de la Loire, Muscadet itself, and the most common (and thus most well-known) variety, Muscadet Sevre-et-Maine, are the four appellations for Muscadet. From the mouth of the Loire Estuary to the western outskirts of Angers, which marks the beginning of the Anjou district, the territory encompassed by these titles is roughly 55 miles (90 km). The majority of the vineyards are located along the banks of the local rivers, the Loire and its tributaries, and to the south and east of Nantes.

Since Melon de Bourgogne is not a particularly delicious grape variety, Muscadet wines run the risk of becoming overly simple and uninteresting if proper attention is not taken in the vineyard and during the winemaking process. This is especially true in warmer vintages, when the severe heat deprives the grapes of their natural acidity and potential complexity.

On the other hand, because the Loire has one of France's wettest and coldest growing seasons, farmers typically aim for complete maturity rather than acid retention.

Many Muscadet wines are left sur lie (or "on the lees") for weeks or even months in order to extract as much flavor and character as possible from the grape must. This prolonged contact with the lees enhances the overall taste profile and gives the wines a richer, creamier texture. Standard and sur lie variations are produced for every Muscadet appellation.

An excellent Muscadet features notes of apple and lemon, occasionally complemented by faint spices and even a tinge of saline that draws attention to the seaside setting of the Nantais. The best specimens also contain an undercurrent of minerality, which is commonly believed to be a reflection of the chalky soils found in the top vines producing Muscadet.

Muscadet Coteaux de la Loire

One of the four Muscadet appellations that dominate wine production in the Pays Nantais section of the Loire Valley, located on the central western coast of France, is Muscadet Coteaux de la Loire. This 1936 title only includes white wines from the region east and northeast of Nantes, all the way to the western border of Anjou.

The wines are made from Melon de Bourgogne, just like all Muscadettes. Under the Coteaux d'Ancenis appellation, red, white, and rosé wines are also produced in the same region. Whites are created from Malvoisie, not Melon, and reds from Gamay.

Not nearly as plentiful as Sèvre-et-Maine, to the south, are the Coteaux de la Loire. Only about 35 to 40 companies annually generate about 800,000 bottles.

This particular terroir is ideal for producing Muscadet wines. The soils, which are a mix of metamorphic, alluvial, and volcanic, are rich in potassium, magnesium, and calcium, giving the grapes the nutrients they need for healthy growth.

Moreover, the combination of limestone, granite, and gravelly soils in the western Loire Valley provides the vineyards with effective drainage, which is essential given the region's moist marine environment. But the clay content, especially near the Loire itself, causes fluctuations in the rate of drainage. Therefore, choosing the right site is crucial to guaranteeing crop quality.

Coteaux de la Loire wines are frequently kept sur lie, or "on the lees," for a few weeks or even months, much like the wines of Muscadet. This enhances the overall flavor profile of the wines and gives them a richer, creamier texture.

The process of validating an area surrounding the village of Champtoceaux as a "Cru Communal" is ongoing as of 2019. The Côteaux de Loire would see its first one here. As of 2019, there were seven such crus in the Sèvre-et-Maine zone, and two more were planned.

Muscadet Sèvre-et-Maine

The most well-known Muscadet appellation in the Pays Nantais region of the Loire Valley, on the country's central west coast, is Muscadet Sèvre-et-Maine. Only white wines from vineyards located southeast and east of Nantes, near the Sèvre Nantaise river and its branch, La Maine, at the western edge of the Loire region, are included in the designation.

As the name implies, Melon de Bourgogne, a grape variety imported to the western Loire from Burgundy, is the only ingredient used to make Muscadet Sèvre-et-Maine. There might occasionally be confusion because of the resemblance between the names Muscadet and Muscat. However, one sip of a crisp, dry Muscadet wine will prove beyond a doubt that it is not derived from the infamously fragrant (and frequently sugary) Muscat varietal.

The appellation is named for the Sèvre-et-Maine region, which is located southeast of Nantes. With over 8,000 hectares (19,000 acres) of vineyards providing wine to about 600 producers, it is a highly cultivated zone.

Because of the appellation's perfect topography for Melon de Bourgogne agriculture, around 80% of all Muscadet wine is produced there. Because of the quantity of potassium, magnesium, and calcium deposits brought about by alluvial soil types, vines have access to the nutrients they need for healthy growth.

Soil drainage is essential in the damp, maritime environment of the western Loire Valley. The area's chalky limestone soils and gravels supply this. Site selection is crucial since clay deposits can also be found along riverbanks, causing variations in drainage rates.

The chalky limestone soils of the region are generally believed to represent an underlying minerality seen in the best Sèvre-et-Maine.

Since Melon de Bourgogne is not a particularly delicious grape variety, Muscadet wines run the risk of being overly simple and uninteresting if care is not taken in the vineyard and during the winemaking process. This is especially true in warmer vintages, when the severe heat deprives the grapes of their natural acidity and potential complexity.

On the other hand, because the Loire has one of France's wettest and coldest growing seasons, farmers typically aim for complete maturity rather than acid retention.

After fermentation, many Muscadet Sèvre-et-Maine wines are left sur lie, or "on the lees," for several weeks or even months in order to extract as much flavor and character as possible from the grape must. This prolonged contact with the lees enhances the overall taste profile and gives the wines a richer, creamier texture.

Crus Communaux

Ten sub regional titles, or "crus," are also included in the Muscadet Sèvre-et-Maine appellation as of the time of writing. These are subzones denoting the greatest terroirs within the larger appellation boundaries rather than single-vineyard designations. The three titles that comprised the tier's inception in 2011 were Clisson, Le Pallet, and Gorges.

Rosé de Loire

Rosé de Loire allows growers to use the whole spectrum of Loire red types, covering much of the area of the 'traditional' Loire Valley.

The official appellation label for still, fresh, dry rosé wines produced in the western French area of the Loire Valley is Rosé de Loire. Rosé de Loire wines are often salmon in color, round, crisp, and mildly fragrant. These kinds of wines are generally meant to be drunk soon.

In 1974, the title was created.

Whereabouts

The Rosé de Loire designation, in general, spans the greater valley of the Loire River from Blois in the east, practically to Nantes on the Atlantic coast in the west. Regarding appellation, the title encompasses the same territory as Touraine,

Saumur, and Anjou; however, it ends at the western boundary with Muscadet.

The Rosé de Loire designation does not include the Coteaux du Loir en Vendômois, the eastern Cheverny, or the Central Loire (which includes regions like Sancerre, Pouilly, and Menetou-Salon).

Climate and geography

This vast area has a diverse range of topography, from the rolling hills of Saumur and Vouvray composed of chalk and tuffeau, a unique blend of limestone and clay, to the shale-based vineyards of Anjou. A large range of soil types are found in the touraine region alone, which includes clay-limestone, clay-flint, and sand or light gravel on tuffeau.

Water has a major impact on the region's climate. The Loire River and its tributaries moderate extremely hot and cold temperatures, while the

Atlantic Ocean (Bay of Biscay) to the west is the source of many of the region's weather patterns.

Varieties of grapes

Rosé de Loire wines may only contain Cabernet Franc, Cabernet Sauvignon, Gamay, Grolleau, Grolleau Gris, Pineau d'Aunis, and Pinot Noir. The winemaker has the final say over which combination (or single variety) to utilize.

The region in which the wines are made typically determines which of the aforementioned red grapes are used (Grolleau Gris, which is regarded as a "gray-skinned" grape, is the lone exception). Anjou, for instance, is largely Cabernet Franc, Cabernet Sauvignon, Grolleau and Grolleau Gris territory while in Touraine, Grolleau is likely to be a prominent component.

While Pineau d'Aunis and Pinot Noir are more uncommon, Gamay is more common in the area. It is important to remember, too, that large wineries or négociants can very easily create wines from any number of grapes, from all across the region, in appellations this size.

Manufacturing

The wines are deemed dry according to production regulations, meaning that their alcohol content cannot exceed 12.5 percent by volume and they cannot have more than three grams of residual sugar per liter.

Additional rosés in the vicinity

The Rosé de Loire title encompasses a significant portion of the region's rosé output, yet it's important to note that each appellation within the title is able to make its own rosé. Cabernet Franc or Sauvignon can be used to produce rosé under the Saumur or Anjou appellations; these must be labeled as "Cabernet de Saumur" or "Cabernet d'Anjou," respectively.

Furthermore, the production standards for Rosé d'Anjou, another potential rosé title in Anjou, are essentially the same as those for Rosé de Loire.

Touraine is classified as a red, white, and rosé wine region; however, the grape varietals found here are mainly limited to Gamay, Cabernet Franc, Cabernet Sauvignon, and Cot (the region's term for Malbec).

History

The region's production of rosé has significantly increased recently, despite the wine's commercial beginnings dating back to the early 1900s, when it was known as "Vin Gris" in Touraine and "Rouget" in Anjou.

While there is historical evidence of winemakers imitating the manufacture of clairet, a rosé wine commonly created as a by-product of red wine production, as seen in Bordeaux, the production of rosé wine does not occur in significant quantities until the 20th century.

Local producers started to advocate for appellation status in the early 1970s, and on September 4, 1974, the Rosé de Loire title was formally created.

Touraine Region

AOC of France and designated wine district, Touraine is located in the very center of the Loire Valley wine region. Located exactly midway between Nantes, the home of Muscadet, and Sancerre, is the city of Tours, which serves as its principal economic hub.

The region of Touraine has its own generic appellation. This has over 5000 hectares (12,350 acres) of officially recognized vineyards spread across the entire district.

The area stretches around 100 kilometers (60 miles) along the Loire river, from Blois in the east to Bourgueil and Chinon in the west. The river continues past this point into the nearby Anjou neighborhood.

Grape varietals and wine styles

The Touraine regional appellation allows for the production of white, red, rosé, or sparkling wines. Of the total production, whites make up 59%, reds 22%, rosé 8%, and sparkling 11%.

Most white wines are made from Sauvignon Blanc, which makes up 43% of all Touraine plantings. At 7%, Chenin Blanc is a far distant second. Up to 20 percent of mixes may contain up to 3 percent of vineyard acreage dedicated to Chardonnay.

A tiny bit of Arbois (or Orbois) is also planted here; historically, it was the most widely grown variety in the département of Loir et Cher, which includes a portion of the Touraine zone. A few vineyards also grow Sauvignon Gris.

Gamay leads the red grape rivals; it makes up 21% of Touraine's vineyard acreage. Reduced amounts of Cabernet Sauvignon and Pinot Noir are also found in red wines made from Cabernet Franc and Malbec, referred to as Côt.

Touraine rosés make up around 10% of the total output. Their style is arid. In addition to the aforementioned grape varietals, Pinot Meunier and the less popular Grolleau Noir and Pineau d'Aunis are also utilized. Pinot Gris may also have an impact.

Within its boundaries, there are also a number of appellations that are more particular in terms of location and wine taste. These include the variegated whites of Vouvray and Montlouis as well as the dry, fruity reds of Bourgueil, Saint-Nicolas de Bourgueil, and Chinon. Maps and wine lists frequently combine the Cheverny and Cour-Cheverny zones, which are located in the hinterland between Tours and Orleans, under the larger Touraine region.

Within the AOC Touraine, producers may additionally add a geographic suffix to five classifications. The regions in question are Touraine Azay-le-Rideau, Touraine-Amboise, -Chenonceaux, -Mesland, and -Oisly.

Touraine's terroir

Touraine is situated roughly 225 kilometers (140 miles) from both the northern Massif Central highlands of central France and the Atlantic Ocean. This leads to a climate that is halfway between continental and marine.

The Touraine vineyards are not particularly cooled by the leisurely pace of the Loire throughout the summer. The area is renowned for its steaming summer days.

Nonetheless, there is a discernible difference in Touraine's wintertime temperatures. Winters in the eastern side of the district are often cooler and drier. They are typically milder and slightly wetter in the west of the area.

Types of soil

Better vineyard sites in the Touraine are those endowed with tuffeau-rich, free-draining soils. This region of the Loire Valley is renowned for its calcareous rock, known as tuffeau. The majority of the well-known châteaux in the valley were constructed using it. Long-term wine aging and storage have also been found to be ideal in Tuffeau caves.

The rock found here in the middle Loire is a type of soft, porous limestone that originated during the Turonian age (called after Tours) of the Cretaceous period, around 90 million years ago. There are several etymologies and confusions involving the terms tuffeau, tuff, and tufa.

Chalkier, stiffer tuffeau blanc and softer, sandier tuffeau jaune are its two main variations. While the latter is the foundation of Saumur's greatest Cabernet Franc grapes in the Loire, the former is utilized to build châteaux. Geologically speaking, these varieties differ from the volcanic rock that Tufo, in southern Italy, grows grapes on

Subregions of Touraine

Bourgueil

Bourgueil, located about halfway between Tours and Angers, is one of Loire's classic Cabernet Franc wines.

In the French Loire Valley wine region, the appellation Bourgueil is used to identify red wines from the commune of the same name as well as six others that surround it. Cabernet Franc is typically used to make all of the wines.

Region encompassed

While officially included in the Touraine district (established by the city of Tours' political limits), Bourgueil differs significantly from its surrounding communities. Chinon, which is located just over the Loire River, and the nearby Saint-Nicolas de Bourgueil are frequently included in the same group as it.

Actually, Bourgueil encompasses both its own appellation and the municipality of Saint-Nicolas. The single factor that distinguishes production regulations from one another is terroir.

Types of wine

A tiny amount of rosé is produced in Bourgueil, one of the relatively few Loire appellations that mostly produces red wines. Both wines are distinguished by their crisp, refreshing acidity and pronounced spiced fruit aromas. Pencil shavings and raspberries are frequently mentioned in tasting notes for Bourgueil reds.

Types of grapes

In the case of the reds, at least 90% of the blend must be Cabernet Franc (appellation regulation allows for up to 10% Cabernet Sauvignon). Particularly well suited to this area's free-draining soils and mild, coastal climate is Cabernet Franc.

Silky, mid-bodied wines with rich notes of undergrowth, spice, and luscious berry fruit are among the varieties available, ranging from light-bodied, fruit-driven styles that are not dissimilar to superb Beaujolais.

Terrain, temperature, and soils

Bourgueil reds are a powerful representation of the soil in which the vines are cultivated, in keeping with the very French concept of terroir. Two soil key types are abundant in the region surrounding Bourgueil and Chinon, and both are ideal for growing fine Cabernet Franc wines.

Styles with fresher, lighter fruit and licorice and red berry aromas are produced from the gravelly alluvial soils near the banks of the Loire. Rich in the native "tuffeau jaune" stone variety, these wines have spicy notes and are fuller, with leather and fur scents.

Named for Touraine, the Turonian epoch, approximately 90 million years ago produced the yellowish, fragile, sedimentary rock known as tuffeau, which is a feature of the Loire region. The rock, which is made up of sea fossils and sand, is incredibly porous; water absorbs quickly and spreads slowly. Because they keep reserves that prevent the vines from completely shutting down during dry spells, and because they drain surplus water from vine roots, these characteristics are perfect for viticulture.

History

The local term for Cabernet Franc is Breton, much as Chenin Blanc has its own name in the Loire region (Pineau). This monk who is credited with popularizing the variety in the 17th century—rather than the region of Bretagne, which is immediately to the northwest—is the context here.

An iconic red wine of the Loire Valley was first produced by local vine-growers who took their cue from Abbot Breton of Bourgueil Abbey, who planted and cared for his Cabernet Franc vines with such meticulousness.

Cheverny

In the heart of France's Loire Valley wine region, the appellation Cheverny is used for both red and white wines. In March 1993, it was elevated from VDQS classification.

The Gamay and Pinot Noir foundations give rise to the crisp, light Cheverny reds. Malbec, known locally as Côt, and Cabernet Franc can be used as supporting wines. It is advisable to eat them within two years of the vintage.

For rosé blends to be made, pinot noir must make up at least 60% of the ingredients. Gamay and a tiny bit of Côt and Cabernet Franc can be used to balance it.

Previously used to make Cheverny rosés, the less popular grape varietals Pineau d'Aunis and Grolleau Noir were used. Similar to several other Loire appellations, they have now been phased out.

'Sauvignon' forms the basis of most white Cheverny wines. This could be a blend of Sauvignon Gris and Sauvignon Blanc. Chardonnay, Chenin Blanc, and Arbois (spelled Orbois here) in smaller quantities are allowed.

Their character is not too distant from that of Pouilly-Fumé and Sancerre wines. They do not, however, have the characteristic minerality and searing Sauvignon acidity that characterize the two most well-known appellations in the eastern Loire.

An estimated 2.7 million liters of red, white, and rosé wines are produced year by about 40 wine growers. These are composed of around 1,418 acres (574 hectares) of vines spread across 23 neighboring parishes on the southern banks of the Loire as well as Cheverny itself.

The white wines of the Cour-Cheverny appellation, which are made from Romorantin, are very different. Nonetheless, they come from a region that has a larger Cheverny catchment area.

Chinon

The appellation Chinon refers to wines made in the region of the central Loire Valley's historic town of Chinon. Although all three types of wine are produced in this region, red wines are currently the main focus, having been for many centuries.

Profile of flavor

The Cabernet Franc grape variety produces the tannic, green, berry-scented, classic Chinon wine. Only 10% of the appellation's total production is made up of white and rosé wines, with small amounts of crisp white Chenin Blanc wines also produced.

Location of the vineyard

Within the administrative department of Indre-et-Loire, Chinon covers 26 communes. Situated on the southern (right) bank of the Loire river as it flows east to west, the territory is near the western end of the department and is concentrated around Chinon town for a radius of about 20 km (12 miles).

Sitting on each side of the northwest-flowing Vienne river, which passes through Chinon town en route to join the Loire on the very western border of the Indre-et-Loire, the Chinon vineyard area also straddles the western end of the Touraine appellation. Additionally, Chinon is located in the Maine-et-Loire department just a few kilometers west of the easternmost vineyards of the neighboring region, Anjou.

Red wine emphasis

Chinon and its neighbor Bourgueil (located on the northern side of the Loire river to Chinon) are somewhat isolated from the rest of the Touraine due to their great emphasis on red wines. As a result, the two are sometimes grouped together with neighboring Saumur (and especially Saumur-Champigny), which is located in Maine-et-Loire just across the administrative border and is one of the few Loire wine growing zones that places a significant focus on red wine.

Profile of flavor
The style of red wines from Chinon ranges from fruity and light-bodied (think of superb Beaujolais in many aspects) to heavier wines with nuanced notes of spiced blackberries, pencil shavings, and undergrowth, and well-structured tannins. The latter type could be likened to Bordeaux wines from the colder regions that are dominated by Franc.

Crisp and pleasant with tastes of spiced fruit, Chinon rosés are ideal for hot summertime picnics by the Vienne or Loire. Similar to the reds, they are almost exclusively composed of Cabernet Franc, while the appellation regulations allow for up to 10% of Cabernet Sauvignon to be grown in the vineyards.

Varieties of grapes

Regarding wine composition, Chinon is one of the more basic appellations, with Cabernet Franc classified as the primary varietal for both red and rosé wines. As mentioned before, Cabernet Sauvignon can make up to 10% of any red wine vineyard. Its percentage in any red or rosé mix does not have to be specified, but it always needs to be in the minority.

Only Chenin Blanc can be used to make White Chinon wines.

Soils Chinon reds are highly influenced by the soil in which the vines were grown, in keeping with the traditional French concept of terroir. There are basically three main types of soils in the Chinon area.

While the hillside locations rich in the indigenous "tuffeau jaune" create more full-bodied, darker, richer, spicier wines with higher cellaring potential, the gravel-sand and clay-sand soils along the Loire yield lighter, fresher styles.

The aforementioned tuffeau is a type of yellowish sedimentary rock that is unique to the Loire region. It originated during the Turonian age, called for Touraine, some 90 million years ago. This delicate rock, which is made up of marine fossils and sand, is very porous, absorbing water quickly but releasing it slowly.

Because it removes surplus moisture from vine roots during wet seasons and releases essential water reserves during dry spells, this is perfect for high-quality viticulture. It is also essential to the terroir of Saumur, which is nearby.

History
Chinon's position as a major trading port on the Vienne river, just upstream from its confluence with

the Loire, suggests that the region's viticulture probably dates back to the Gallo-Roman era.

Wine was first mentioned in the area in the eleventh century, according to a local figure's biography named Saint Mexme. The story tells of a landowner in Chinon who decided to ship his wine to Nantes by boat in an attempt to gain a higher price for it.

The wines of Chinon were found at courts throughout the Plantagenet dynasty's ascent to the English throne in the late 12th and early 13th centuries (the family originated in the region). From its native South West/Bordeaux region, the Cabernet Franc variety is said to have already reached the region. It is thought to have done so via boat along the coast to Nantes, from which it derived its antiquated synonym, Breton, and then up the Loire river.

Born in Chinon, the Renaissance scholar and playwright Francois Rabelais greatly enhanced the fame of the region's wines. "I know where Chinon lies, and the painted wine cellar also, having myself drunk there many a glass of cool wine," declares Pantagruel, the play's title character.

Even Cabernet Franc is mentioned by Rabelais in his book Gargantua (Book I, chapter 13): "this good Breton wine, which doesn't grow in Brittany but in the good land of Véron [the Chinon region]". Chinon and Tours both have statues of Rabelais, and the Université Francois Rabelais in the area bears his name.

Present circumstances and output

In July 1937, Chinon was initially designated as an appellation, with 550 hectares (1460 acres) of vines at that time. Presently, the area has 2400 hectares (5900 acres) of vineyard, approximately 170 winegrowers, and produces 10 million liters of wine a year on average.

Approximately 84% of the production is dedicated to red wines, with rosé making up 12% and white wines making up the remaining 4%.

Long-lived

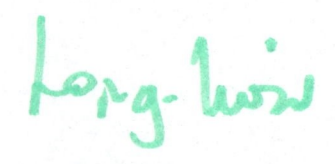

Montlouis

In the middle Loire Valley of France, the commune of Montlouis-sur-Loire produces still, sparkling, dry, and sweet white wines under the appellation Montlouis. All of them are based on the main white wine grape in this region of France, Chenin Blanc, also referred to as Pineau de la Loire locally.

International wine markets are not very familiar with the Montlouis moniker or the town's wines. Just to the north on the opposite side of the Loire, Vouvray, Montlouis's more well-known sister appellation, dwarfs them. In fact, the wines of the commune were marketed and sold as Vouvray until the 1938 establishment of the Montlouis appellation.

The exceptional longevity of high-quality Montlouis wine is one of its primary attributes. Even though mature bottles often have an overtly honeyed taste, many still have an enticing olfactory freshness after over thirty years.

This is mainly because Chenin Blanc has a strong acidity by nature, which acts as a preservative to keep the wine from going bad. Chenin's highly fragrant makeup is also essential. When the wines are young, they have notes of acacia blossom, quince, and green apples; as they age, they develop notes of honeysuckle, quince, and lanolin.

Similar to Vouvray, Montlouis does not have an established, effective system for labeling its wines that would help differentiate them from one another. Generally speaking, its wines can be categorized as sweet, dry, still, or sparkling. The phrases sec, sec-tendre, demi-sec, and moelleux are theoretically allowed on the labels; however, only Sec and Moelleux are actually used frequently. The amount of residual sugar in any Montlouis wine classified sec is less than 8 grams per liter. The sweetest wines are called moelleux wines, which can have 50 to over 200 grams per liter (see Montlouis Moelleux).

The same is true with Montlouis sparkling wines, which have two different label designations: mousseux (completely sparkling) and petillant (spritzy), adjectives that are far too infrequently used on labels. In actuality, there is no legally recognized technical distinction between mousseux and petillant, which may account for why manufacturers seem to use the more general and commercially appealing term "methode traditionnelle." Thankfully, the foil-wrapped, wire-secured cork that is typical of sparkling wines worldwide makes Montlouis sparkling wines quite straightforward to identify on the store. Regarding details on these wines specifically, see Montlouis Petillant - Mousseux.

The vineyards surrounding Montlouis have terroir that is characterized by gravelly, free-draining topsoils with a deep bed of tuffeau. This type of calcareous rock is found in the central Loire, especially near Saumur and in the vicinity of Vouvray and Montlouis.

Approximately 90 million years ago, during the Cretaceous period, soft, porous limestone called tuffeau was created. The two main varieties are softer, sandier tuffeau jaune and challier, harder tuffeau blanc. Tuffeau's porosity provides a perfect balance between water retention and drainage, protecting vines from drought and waterlogging alike.

The Atlantic Ocean is located 225 kilometers (140 miles) away from Montlouis, hence the climate there is in between maritime and continental. The topography is variable enough to cause fluctuation in the local meso climates, even though it is not as complex as that of Burgundy or Alsace.

Valençay

The name Valençay is applied to red, white, and rosé wines that are primarily produced in the region north of the town of Valençay, which is located in the administrative department of the Indre in western France. After 34 years as a VDQS, the title was elevated to full AOC rank in March 2004.

The red wines are made from Gamay, Cabernet Sauvignon, Pinot Noir, and Côt, which is the term for Malbec in the region. They are best enjoyed within a few years following harvest and are made utilizing customary local winemaking methods.

The fact that Sauvignon Blanc is the main varietal used to make Valençay white wines indicates that this region is closer to the eastern edge of the Loire, even though Sancerre and Pouilly are still more than 100 kilometers (60 miles) to the east. Chardonnay, Sauvignon Gris, and the very uncommon Arbois grape variety—which should not be mistaken with the Arbois appellation—are also allowed in the white mixes.

As expected, rosés made under the Valençay appellation often include a foundation of Malbec, Gamay, and Pinot Noir, however they can also combine approved red and white varietals.

To the northwest, it is situated slightly beyond the Touraine district. Alternatively, it is occasionally categorized as a component of the Upper Loire Valley wine area. The Cher, a tributary of the Loire, passes through some of Valencay's vineyards, however this is only true of those in the north. The Loire river is actually located more than 50 kilometers (30 miles) north of Valençay.

Growing in chilly climates with clay, limestone, and flint-based soils, Valençay wines are more often crisp and refreshing than complicated and structured. Currently, only 100 hectares (250 acres) of vines, held by a relatively limited number of growers, are used to make the appellation's wines.

Valençay cheese is the area's most well-known product. This is produced all over the province of Berry. It is a goat's milk cheese that hasn't been pasteurized and has a charcoal-dusted rind. In 1998, it obtained its AOC.

Vouvray

The most well-known and esteemed appellation in the Touraine growing region of the Loire Valley is Vouvray. The title encompasses white Chenin Blanc wines from eight villages surrounding the medieval town of Vouvray on the northern banks of the Loire River. The wines are classified as sweet wine, dry, still, sparkling, and blended.

The flagship wine of the Chenin Blanc grape, sometimes known as Pineau de la Loire there, is Vouvray; Savennieres and the Anjou sweet whites follow closely behind. Chenin is used in only a few wine regions worldwide. None highlight the flavors and scents of the variety with as much diversity and emphasis.

France produces significantly less Chenin Blanc annually than South Africa does. Vouvray's textural balance and aromatic complexity are only found in the finest South African Chenin Blancs.

In actual usage, Chenin Blanc is nearly usually utilized by itself. Permitted as well, Menu Pineau, often known as Arbois, was historically used to counterbalance the acidity of Chenin Blanc. On the official Vouvray AOP website, it isn't noted, though, because it is so uncommon.

Since the Middle Ages, the vines in the Vouvray area have produced fine white wines. 'Vouvray' was, predictably, one of France's very first official appellation titles, having been established shortly after the INAO was established in 1936.

Considering the variety of styles covered by the Vouvray appellation, it's astonishing that after all this time, it has managed to stay a single label. Ultimately, the appellation system's primary purpose is to inform consumers of the exact type of wine they are purchasing.

Styles of Vouvray

Though one of the most respected names in the Loire, vouvray is also arguably one of the most ambiguous, especially when it comes to sweetness levels. While its winemakers are allowed to use numerous formal names (Sec, Sec-Tendre, Demi-Sec, and Moelleux) to describe the sweetness of their wine, these terms are rarely used on labels. Here, Sec is the only legally mandated label phrase that needs to be on sparkling Vouvray labels if the wine has less than 8 grams of residual sugar per liter.

Vouvray sparkling wines are easily recognizable on the shelf because of their well-known foil-wrapped and wire-secured cork. However, there are two degrees of sparkle in Vouvray: petillant (spritzy) and mousseux (totally dazzling), in keeping with the appellation's complexity and confusing range of styles. The degree of fizz is frequently as ambiguous on the label as the degree of sweetness.

It is common practice to drop the official terms petillant and mousseux in favor of more identifiable, more commercial terms like brut and méthode traditionelle. See Vouvray Petillant - Mousseux for additional details about sparkling Vouvray.

Vouvray's likelihood of aging

The exceptional longevity of high-quality Vouvray wines is one of their main attributes. Many over-30-year-old bottles frequently exhibit amazing freshness and liveliness. This is mainly because Chenin Blanc has a high acidity by nature, which preserves the wine and lets it age for many years. Chenin's strong aromatic profile, which is resilient enough to endure long aging, is also essential.

Vouvrays are known for their youthful scents of green apples, quince, and acacia blossoms. These develop into tertiary scents with time, including lanolin, quince, and honeysuckle. During its early years, much of Vouvray was harsh and merciless. After about five years, many instances only start to open out and relax into drinkable maturity.

Waiting for a mature, high-quality Vouvray will pay off handsomely. Vouvray is therefore perfect for people who have the time and resources to cellar wine, but for others who don't, it may be confusing or disappointing. This also applies to many other excellent Loire Valley Chenin Blancs, such as the wines of Montlouis, the sister appellation of Vouvray located immediately across the Loire.

Vouvray developing circumstances
The local vignerons maintain that terroir is just as important to the style of these wines as the Chenin Blanc grapes they are created from, as is the case

in many other French wine regions. The tuffeau, a calcareous rock type found in several places in the central Loire, including Saumur and here in Vouvray, is a crucial component of the local terroir.

Approximately 90 million years ago, during the Cretaceous period, soft, porous limestone called tuffeau was created. The two main varieties are softer, sandier tuffeau jaune and challier, harder tuffeau blanc. The volcanic tufa with the same name, which is used for planting grapes in Tufo, southern Italy, is different geologically from both kinds. Tuffeau's porosity provides a perfect balance between water retention and drainage, protecting vines from drought and waterlogging alike.

Despite being a full 225 km/140 miles away from the Atlantic coast, the climate here is in between maritime and continental. The topography is variable enough to cause fluctuation in the local meso climates, even though it is not as obviously complex as it is in Burgundy or Alsace.

Vouvray village is located on a plateau, however the land flow is broken up by several neighboring streams. This results in sheltered south-facing slopes and shallow valleys. The most valuable vineyard locations are found along the town's northern edge, on these slopes.

These tributary streams frequently generate the damp conditions necessary for grapes to be affected by noble rot (botrytis cinerea). Weather that is both warm and humid raises the risk of botrytis. Years that are colder and drier are better for dry and sparkling styles.

Vouvray and Savennières, the other Chenin Blanc specialties of the Loire, are very similar. Although there is a distance of 110 km (70 miles) between these two small wine villages, they are both situated right outside the main town of their respective wine districts, Tours and Angers.

Above deep tuffeau, the vineyards of Vouvray and Savennieres benefit from gravelly, free-draining topsoils. Savennieres wines are primarily dry, still wines (though they were formerly much sweeter), whilst Vouvray has managed to hold onto its own characteristics.

Upper Loire Region

The wine districts of the Loire Valley located upriver (to the south and east) of Touraine are collectively referred to as Upper Loire, an informal term. It combines the most well-known Loire appellations, Sancerre and Pouilly-Fumé, with several lesser-known ones, including Côtes du Forez, Menetou-Salon, Quincy, and Valencay.

The notion of a "Upper Loire" sub-region is required since the appellations that make up this sub-region are not categorized according to an administrative or historical territory; rather, their shared characteristic is their closeness to the Loire River, which is the longest in France. The majority of other French wine regions, like Alsace, Bourgogne, Champagne, and Provence, closely align with a department or administrative region.

A Loire administrative department does exist, but it's located 30 km (20 miles) west of Lyon, hundreds of kilometers upstream from the center of the Loire Valley wine area. Ironically, Côte Roannaise and Côtes du Forez, two of the least well-known Loire Valley appellations, are located there.

They are the only duo on the Loire that focus on Gamay-based red and rosé wines. They share more characteristics with Beaujolais, which is located only 50 km/30 miles to the east, due to its sandy and granitic soils and similar wine style, than they do with any other Loire appellation.

The Loire runs between Pouilly-sur-Loire and Sancerre, two of France's most renowned wine regions, two hundred kilometers (120 miles) northwest of the Côte Roannaise. Near these two towns, the Pouilly-Fumé and Sancerre appellation labels are virtually solely used to market crisp, aromatic Sauvignon Blanc from the wineries and vineyards in the area.

Their white wines made in Chasselas and marketed under the Pouilly-sur-Loire label are more conventional but far less well-known.

A collection of lesser-known grape lands situated some distance from the river can be found immediately west of Sancerre. Quincy (just Sauvignon Blanc), Valencay, Menetou-Salon, and Reuilly (red, rosé, and white wines made from a variety of varietals) are their appellations.

The Loire passes through the Coteaux du Giennois (the region surrounding the town of Gien), a short distance downstream from Sancerre, and then heads north to Orleans, Touraine, and the center of the Loire Valley wine region.

There is a noticeable distinction between the wines and terroirs of the Upper Loire and those found in Touraine, Anjou, and especially the Pays Nantais lower downstream. A full 200 miles (325 km) east of the Muscadet vineyards is Sancerre, which experiences a drier, nearly continental environment in contrast to the moderate, damp, marine climate of the Muscadet grapes. This is reflected in the wines, which helps to explain (part of) the distinction between the powerful aromatics of Sancerre and the delicate finesse of Muscadet.

In Upper Loire vineyards, especially in Sancerre, Pouilly, and Menetou-Salon, limestone is an essential soil type. Their position in the southernmost point of the Paris Basin is the cause of this. The Paris Basin, a shallow bowl of sedimentary rock that is home to the valuable calcareous soils that the Loire shares with Champagne and northern Burgundy (most notably Chablis, which is only 100 km (60 miles) from

Sancerre), is an important geological zone in northern France. The Upper Loire possesses silex (flint), which these other regions lack.

Flint's exceptional capacity to retain heat and reflect light helps the grapes reach full ripeness, resulting in wines with more body. It is also credited with bringing the smoky quality of the regional Sauvignon Blanc to life, explaining the local appellation Blanc Fumé, which translates to "smoky white."

Subregion of Upper Loire

Côte Roannaise

The appellation Côte Roannaise is used to identify Gamay-based red and rosé wines. Situated in the French administrative region of Auvergne-Rhône-Alpes, to the west of Roanne, are 14 communes that make up the viticultural zone.

The wines rely heavily on their vivid, fresh fruit tastes and have a light body and minimal tannin content. With carbonic maceration, they exhibit all the characteristics of original Gamay, and most are best enjoyed within a few years after vintage.

First established as a VDQS in 1955, the Côte Roannaise appellation was elevated to full AOC status in February 1994. Côtes Roannaise wines are produced on about 180 hectares (445 acres) of vines, all Gamay, that yield about 800,000 liters of wine year. Six out of the bottles contain rosé wines, with red wines making up the remaining percentage.

The terroir of this region is enriched with basalt from volcanic soils, despite being mostly composed of sandy, granitic soils; several Côtes Roannais cuvees have names that allude to this terrain. There is a noticeable continental climate with highly variable daily temperatures and erratic weather patterns.

Similar to the wines of the Côtes du Forez, which are located just to the south, Côte Roannaise wines are hard to categorize as belonging to a larger wine area. The vineyards are in the Auvergne-Rhône-Alpes region, however they are situated along the upper Loire River.

Conversely, Gamay is most recognized for being the grape of Beaujolais, which is located less than 80 kilometers (50 miles) northeast. Furthermore,

Roanne is significantly nearer Macon and Condrieu than it is to Sancerre.

Coteaux du Giennois

Red, white, and rosé wines from 14 parishes surrounding Gien are categorized under the appellation Coteaux du Giennois, formerly known as Côteaux de Gien. This French town is located in the Loire Valley wine area, halfway between Orléans and Sancerre.

Of the total output, over 60% is made up of white wines. These are crisp Sauvignon Blancs, similar in style to those grown in Pouilly and Sancerre, just to the south.

Gamay and occasionally Pinot Noir are used to make the Coteaux du Giennois red wines, which are usually of a light body. A petite amount of pale, peach-scented rosé rounds out the collection.

The best Giennois vines are grown in terroirs that are relatively typical of the 'Upper Loire'. Along the

Loire, vines are grown on silica- or limestone-rich soils, as well as on the former river terraces at Gien.

With continental influences, the climate is temperate, with cold winters and mild summers. Other than being unusual, spring frosts are only a problem in 1991 and 2016.

These vines cover over 205 hectares (470 acres), and they yield about 1 million bottles of wine annually. Not much of this is marketed outside of France.

Côtes du Forez

The appellation Côtes du Forez is used to distinguish red and rosé wines from 17 communes located in the administrative region of Rhône-Alpes in western France. They use just the Gamay variety in their construction.

The wines rely heavily on their vivid, fresh fruit tastes and have a light body and minimal tannin content. They are best enjoyed within a few years after the vintage and have all the characteristics of a traditional Gamay vinified through carbonic maceration. Thus, the style is extremely close to that of Beaujolais, which is located less than 50 miles (80 km) northeast.

In February 2000, the Côtes du Forez appellation—which had initially been established as a VDQS in 1953—was elevated to full AOC designation. About 200 acres, or 120 hectares, are planted with grapes, yielding fewer than 450,000 liters of wine annually.

There is one rosé wine in every five bottles, with red wines making up the remaining percentage.

The terroir in the Forez region is enriched with basalt from volcanic soils, despite the area's predominance of sandy, granitic soils. Numerous cuvées from the Côtes du Forez have names that evoke this region. With its wide variations in temperature throughout the day and erratic weather patterns, the climate is unmistakably continental.

Similar to the wines of the Côte Roannaise, which are produced here, these wines also have a bit of an identity dilemma. For a large number of wine vendors and buyers, who are accustomed to categorizing wineries into broader geographic areas, this is the case. These vineyards are situated between the upper reaches of the Loire River and the Auvergnen Monts du Forez hills.

Many people are surprised to learn that the Loire exists here in the southeast of central France, which is essentially Rhône wine country. The final 400 kilometers (250 miles) of the river, which connects Pouilly-sur-Loire to the Atlantic Ocean, are the parts of it that are most well-known.

Vines from the Côtes du Forez are grown near the banks of the Loire, yet within the official territory of Rhône-Alpes, and even within the department named 'Loire'. This strangely also applies to Saint-Joseph and Condrieu, which are located 40 kilometers distant on the Rhône. All in all, these elements along with the style and variety of the grapes make it extremely difficult to categorize the Côtes du Forez as a distinct wine region.

Menetou-Salon

At the easternmost point of France's Loire Valley wine region sits the village of Menetou-Salon. Its appellation applies to Pinot Noir and Sauvignon Blanc-based white, red, and rosé wines.

Approximately 500 hectares (1,235 acres) of vines, distributed among 11 parishes surrounding the settlement, are currently under the Menetou-Salon appellation. The majority—about 80%—is planted to Sauvignon Blanc. Each year, about 1.8 million liters of white wine, 750,000 liters of red wine, and 100,000 liters of rosé are produced.

Kimmeridgian limestone sediment makes up soils. The Central Loire region experiences a moderate climate with continental influences and significant seasonal temperature changes. While seldom common, spring frosts can be dangerous.

Seen by many as a possible competitor to its immediate northeast neighbor, the renowned Sancerre appellation, Menetou-Salon is quickly making a name for itself internationally. The crisp, refreshing Sauvignon Blanc and light, fruit-driven Pinot Noir wines from this appellation are from very similar terroirs and are frequently less expensive than comparable wines branded as Sancerre.

But this is hardly a brand-new area. The wines were noted for their quality as early as the middle of the fourteenth century, and monastic viticulture probably began in the eleventh century.

Pouilly-Fumé

A dry white wine produced from Sauvignon Blanc grapes, Pouilly-Fumé is highly regarded in the Loire Valley. In this sense, it's only competitors are Vouvray and Sancerre, which is located across the Loire River.

Blanc Fumé de Pouilly was the initial name of the 1937-created Pouilly-Fumé appellation. At the same time, the village's Chasselas-based wines were awarded the Pouilly-sur-Loire title.

The name Pouilly-Fumé consists of two parts. The village where the wines are produced, Pouilly-sur-Loire, is short for Pouilly. Fume is a portmanteau for Blanc Fumé, the colloquial term for Sauvignon Blanc in the area. Understandably, Pouilly-Fuissé, a southern Burgundy wine with a Chardonnay base, is occasionally confused with it.

On the Loire's right bank, Pouilly-Fumé's recognized viticultural region consists of seven parishes. These stretch a few miles northward to Saint-Martin-sur-Nohain from Mesves-sur-Loire in the south. Technically speaking, these villages are in Burgundy, but Pouilly-Fumé is still distinctly a "Loire Valley" wine.

Wine style and organoleptic characteristics
The word "smoky" in French is fumé, as in Blanc. It refers to the aroma of striking gunflint that is typical of the Sauvignon Blanc wines grown in the area. A common term for this unique scent is pierre à fusil, which translates to "flint" or "rifle stone." For the winemakers of Pouilly-Fumé, it is a crucial point of distinction and a major source of pride in the community.

Pouilly-Fumé wines are among the liveliest in France when it comes to aroma, though generally they are not as overbearing as the famously grassy varieties of Sauvignon Blanc made in New Zealand, especially Marlborough. They smell of green fruit (lime, green apple, gooseberry) with a bright streak of fragrances, backed by smoky flint, slate, and wet wool.

Many producers began adding wood to their Pouilly-Fumé wines in the 1980s, either through barrel fermentation, barrel maturation, or both. The resultant wines were more complex in terms of scent and texture than the typical unoaked wines, and they were also more appropriate for medium-term cellaring. The majority of contemporary Pouilly-Fumé will age better in a bottle for three to six years.

Grape varietals and terroir

As is customary in France, the unique flavor and scent of Pouilly-Fumé are attributed to the terroir of the region. It has undergone extensive study and mapping. The main categories of soil types include clays with different compositions, marlstone, limestone, and the crucial flint.

The most crucial elements are flint and limestone. In this mild growing season, both offer outstanding light- and heat-reflecting qualities that aid in the vines reaching their ideal ripeness. Didier Dagueneau, a legendary winemaker in the area, even called one of his best bottlings "Silex." This is a combination of flinty clay, limestone, and silica.

The majority of the grapes grown in the vineyards in Pouilly-sur-Loire were Gamay and Pinot Noir until phylloxera destroyed large areas of vines in the 1860s. Sauvignon Blanc proved to be more receptive to grafting than these red varietals when the answer to the phylloxera outbreak was discovered—grafting European vines onto American rootstocks. Sauvignon became the most commonly planted grape variety in Pouilly as a result.

The entire vineyard area and Pouilly-Fumé's popularity increased significantly in the 1970s and 1980s. The Chasselas were displaced when Sauvignon Blanc vines were planted in the area. Pouilly-Fumé vines currently occupy about 1325 hectares (3275 acres) as of 2005. This is in contrast to about 74 acres, or 30 ha, of Chasselas.

The yield range for vineyards is 6500–7500 liters per hectare. There must be at least 6000 vines planted per hectare. Over the past five years, the average yearly production has been approximately 7 million liters (1.85 million US gallons).

Sancerre

Renowned for its crisp and fragrant white wines produced from Sauvignon Blanc, Sancerre is a tiny wine district located in central France. It's also well-known for its superior goat cheeses, which go wonderfully with the regional wine.

Situated atop a bean-shaped hill overlooking the river Loire, the town of the same name is surrounded by vineyards. The only time that "Sancerre" has been so closely linked with white wines is since the middle of the 20th century, when an appellation was established to preserve it.

The district was more well-known for its full-bodied reds before this. Gamay and Pinot Noir were the predominant varietals grown in these vineyards until phylloxera devastated large areas of them in the 1860s. White wines were produced mostly from Chasselas, not Sauvignon, and constituted a small minority.

Vine Sauvignon Blanc proved more resilient than these other kinds when the phylloxera pandemic was solved by grafting European vines onto American rootstocks. As a result, Sauvignon became the grape most frequently planted in Sancerre. This evolution is likely what has made the region and its wines so well-known today.

Even now, only a limited amount of Chasselas is produced in the region, primarily at Pouilly-sur-Loire on the opposite side of the Loire. Red Sancerre Rouge, which is made only from Pinot Noir, makes up less than 20 percent of the district's yearly production.

On the west bank of the Loire, a 15-mile stretch of gently sloping hills is home to the Sancerre wine region. Currently, the area produces wines from over 6970 acres (2820ha) of vineyards, which is about twice as much as when the Sancerre appellation was established in November 1936.

Due to a combination of bad vintages and the highly competitive worldwide wine market, the Loire Valley wine sector has experienced severe economic hardship over the last ten years; nonetheless, Sancerre has not felt as much pressure as other districts. Because of its solid historical standing and the contemporary wine drinker's attraction to its style, Sancerre has managed to hold onto its title of "king of the hill" in the Loire Valley.

Wine type
Gooseberries, grass, nettles, and a faint trace of stony minerality are among the strong aromas of the traditional Sancerre wine, which is white and sharply acidic. Richer, riper examples often have fruitier aromas of passionfruit and lemon peel, especially those from warmer, west-facing areas

with calcareous soils. Generally speaking, Sancerre is less "obvious" than the most well-known New World varieties of Sauvignon Blanc; it is less aggressively citrusy than Casablanca and less grassy than Marlborough.

In Sancerre, about 170,000hl of wine are produced every vintage. Though 22,000hl of red and 12,000hl of rosé, both from Pinot Noir, are also reported annually, the majority of this is white wine.

Terroir

Sancerre is situated hundreds of miles from the westernmost vineyards in the Loire Valley, at the very eastern edge of the region's primary vineyard area. Most vineyards are located between 200 and 400 meters (655 and 1310 feet) above sea level, on hillsides with a good south-facing slope to maximize sun exposure.

In actuality, it is nearer the Côte d'Or in Burgundy than it is to Anjou and Touraine, the other two major wine regions of the Loire. Chablis, the northernmost province of Burgundy, is only 50 miles away. The terroir of Sancerre is influenced by the renowned Kimmeridgian soils of Chablis, especially in the vicinity of Chavignol hamlet.

Types of soil

Similarly, winegrowers in Sancerre take great pride in their soil types. Chalk, limestone-gravel, and silex (flint) are the three primary categories into which they can be classified. The latter is frequently credited with creating the unique, smokey scent of pierre à fusil, or gunflint, that may be detected in some Sauvignon wines from this region of the Loire Valley. Certain Sancerre wines exhibit a distinct scent, particularly those sourced from eastern vines nearer the Loire. This explains the origin of Sauvignon's customary alias, Blanc Fumé, which endures in the appellation of Pouilly-Fumé, Sancerre's neighbor and adversary.

Climate

The region is characterized by a cool continental climate, with the Atlantic Coast about 480 kilometers (300 miles) to the east. Sancerre experiences hot, brief summers and lengthy, harsh winters, with numerous April frosts.

Snowfall is frequent during the winter. April is said to be the driest month, and November receives the most rainfall.

Quincy

East of the Loire wine area in France, the village of Quincy has its own appellation for dry white wines made from Sauvignon Blanc. This is not the actual Loire Valley; rather, it is one of a few appellations in the vicinity of Bourges. Rather of the Loire proper, the Cher river, a tributary of the Loire, passes via Quincy.

The traditional Quincy wine is a crisp, high-acid white wine. Citrus and flowery, grassy flavors are frequently mentioned in tasting comments, and occasionally they are supported by the minerality present in the best Loire Valley wines.

This region has been producing wine for many decades; it peaked right before the phylloxera outbreak in the 1860s. A few months before Sancerre, in August 1936, the parish's wines became the first in the eastern Loire to be officially recognized as AOC wines.

Over the past few decades, Quincy wine has seen a significant growth in popularity. The popularity of the surrounding white wines of Pouilly-Fumé and Sancerre, whose production is very similar, is undoubtedly helping the village. 2018 saw the planting of 308 hectares (761 acres) of Sauvignon Blanc vines in Quincy and Brinay, the commune next door that is also included in the Quincy appellation.

The continental climate is advantageous to the vines in Quincy. Compared to those who grow closer to the Atlantic, they have a far dryer and warmer growth season. The grapes need to be left on the vine for a longer period of time to reach their maximum ripeness because the climate is still chilly worldwide. The wine becomes more nuanced as a result of this slower ripening process. Still, they are often regarded as less refined and more 'rustic' than those from the actual eastern end of the Loire Valley.

Due to the area's location between the Cher and its tributary, the Yèvre, the soils here are a mixture of sand and gravel. These soil types reflect a lot of sunshine and heat up quickly, which helps the vines ripen. The impact is comparable to what is felt in the well-known Graves area. There are some of Bordeaux's best white wines produced, again with a significant amount of Sauvignon Blanc.

Here, on the southern edge of the Paris Basin, there is also a significant concentration of limestone. It can be found in many different forms, such as light clays and solid stones.

Reuilly

The French town of Reuilly is located in the Loire wine region. Its name is used for red wines created from Pinot Noir, rosé made from Pinot Gris and Sauvignon Blanc, and white wines made from Sauvignon Blanc.

Not to be confused with the Loire Valley proper, this appellation is one of a small group around the town of Bourges, including the adjacent Menetou-Salon and Quincy. Rather than the Loire itself flowing past Reuilly, it is the Cher river, a tributary of the Loire.

Since its creation in September 1937, the appellation has steadily and gradually grown. With roughly 259 hectares (495 acres) of vineyards, it currently produces somewhat less than 1.2 million liters of wine annually.

About half of this is white wine, and the other half is divided about equally between rosé and red wine.

The wines are a more reasonably priced option to the region's more well-known brands, such Sancerre. Globally, they are becoming more and more well-known and acknowledged.

Reuilly and its neighboring vineyards enjoy a continental climate, with a growing season that is significantly warmer and dryer than that of regions further downstream near the Atlantic. The climate is still chilly overall, though, so the grapes need to be left on the vine for a longer period of time to ripen fully.

The wines become more nuanced as a result of this slower ripening process. They are, therefore, usually regarded as less refined and more "rustic" than those from the actual eastern Loire Valley.

Here, the topsoils contain a mixture of gravel and sand. The reason for this is that Reuilly is situated between the Cher and the Arnon, two rivers.

These soil types reflect a lot of sunshine and heat up quickly, which helps the vines ripen. This bears resemblance to the renowned Bordeaux region of Graves, whose exquisite white wines are derived from Sauvignon Blanc. The bedrock (the southern edge of the Paris Basin) is mostly composed of limestone.

Refreshing and rich in acidity, the typical Reuilly white wine has grassy, herbaceous aromas that are brightened with citrus overtones. The reds and roses are typical of Pinot Noir from cool climates; they are fruit-driven, light-bodied, and aromatic of violets, raspberries, and cherries.

Similar to the majority of parishes in this area, Reuilly used to produce a significant amount of

Gamay until the 1860s phylloxera outbreak destroyed the crop. While some of that grape type is still farmed here, it is now known by the less fancy (and lengthier) title IGP Coteaux du Cher et de l'Arnon.

Vendée-Poitou Region

The region of western France known as Vendée-Poitou was historically a significant wine region but is now hardly spoken of. It bridges the divide between the far more well-known wine areas of Cognac (to the south) and the Loire Valley (to the north).

The Vendée-Poitou wine region is not a separate entity. Immediately south of the Pays Nantais, the region that is home to Muscadet, lies the administrative department known as Vendée (previously Bas-Poitou). It covered the western half of the old province of Poitou, which was centered on Poitiers, a historic town located to the south of Chinon.

This comparatively vast region extends 240 kilometers (150 miles) inland from the Atlantic coast. This is approximately equivalent to the administrative divisions of Deux Sèvres, Vienne, and Vendée.

The region is seldom acknowledged as a wine region because it is home to only a few wine appellations. The Fiefs Vendéens and Haut-Poitou AOC labels are the most important wine appellations in the region.

Poitou was a more dependable source of wine than Burgundy and Champagne because of its temperate, Atlantic-influenced environment. Because of this, it was the preferred wine location in the early Middle Ages for a number of northern nations, including the present-day United Kingdom, Belgium, The Netherlands, and portions of Scandinavia.

Poitous's performance in these markets was closely correlated with the political and military climate. Throughout the Middle Ages, English and

French sovereignty alternated over its principal harbor town, La Rochelle.

The region's wine exports flourished under English administration (1154–1224 under Henry II and 1360–1372), as well. Bordeaux was another growing wine region, and the English were forced to capitalize on its viticultural potential when La Rochelle was brought back under French administration.

Subregions of vendee-Poitou

Fiefs Vendéens

A small area in the Vendée administrative department on France's central west coast is known as the Fiefs Vendéens. The region is located south of the Pays Nantais and south of the major coastal area of the western Loire Valley wine region. The two growth zones are roughly 70 kilometers (45 miles) apart.

Made in five subzones scattered around the southern half of the Vendée administrative department, the red, white, and rosé wines under the 1984-created Fiefs Vendéens (or "Vendée Fiefdoms") appellation are all produced there. The subzone name must follow the title "Fiefs Vendéens," and labels may also include the term "Val de Loire."

The five grapes that are used to make red and rosé wines are Pinot Noir, Gamay, Cabernet Franc, Cabernet Sauvignon, and Négrette. These are divided into the primary grape (at least 40% of any blend), a "complementary" grape (at least 10% of a blend), and "accessory grapes" for each color, depending on the subzone.

Throughout the reds, which are mostly Cabernet Franc or Pinot Noir depending on the region, négrette takes on a supporting role. Rosés are dominated by Gamay/Pinot Noir, with regional variations in the main varietal.

Chenin Blanc paired with Chardonnay is the main varietal for white wines.

It is preferable to look at each subzone separately due to its dispersed character (technically referred to as "complementary geographic denominations") and unique requirements.

Areas Within the Fiefs Vendées

Just north of Les Sables-d'Olonne, on the Atlantic coast, are five communes that make up Brem. Chenin Blanc is the main varietal used to make white wines; Chardonnay and Grolleau Gris have supporting roles. The majority of red and rosé wines are made from Pinot Noir, while they can also be made from Gamay, Négrette, Cabernet Franc, and Sauvignon.

Mareuil encompasses a collection of eight communes and is located south of La Roche-sur-Yon, the departmental headquarters (préfecture). Here, the white types are mostly Chenin and Chardonnay, while the reds are primarily Cabernet Franc-based.

Négrette may also be included, with minimal contributions permitted from Gamay, Cabernet

Sauvignon, and Pinor Noir. Gamay-based rosés are required, usually paired with Pinot Noir.

Chantonnay is located 19 miles (just over 30 kilometers) east of La Roche-sur-Yon. Mareuil's red and white wine blends are identical in this sizable commune. The majority of rosés are made from Pinot Noir, with a small amount from Gamay and the remaining portion coming from Négrette and the Cabernets.

Situated in the southeast of the department, around 60 kilometers (37 miles) southeast of La Roche-sur-Yon, Pissotte is another single-community designation, situated immediately north of Fontenay-le-Comte. Here, the reds are similar to those of Brem (Pinot Noir dominates with Négrette and the rest playing lesser roles), while the whites are still Chenin Blanc (major) and Chardonnay (minor). Rosé wines have to be primarily created from Gamay, just like Mareuil.

Four communes, the northernmost of which borders Pissotte, are included in Vix's coverage area to the south. Southwest and west of Fontenay-le-Comte are where they are located. Although Chenin Blanc still makes up the majority of the white wines here, with small amounts of Chardonnay, Sauvignon Blanc is also allowed. Reds, like Chatonnay and Mareuil, are dominated by Cabernet Franc, with Négrette taking on a supporting role and, when it's present, Cabernet Sauvignon, Pinot Noir, and Gamay playing lesser parts. Rosés, like Mareuil and Pisotte, are mostly made from Gamay and Pinot Noir.

Geography, History, Climate, and Production

The organoleptic characteristics of the wine made in Fiefs Vendéens are significantly influenced by the maritime climate in this area. Because of their proximity to the Atlantic coast, they are typically fresher, crisper, and have a notable acidity, with a little lower alcohol and sugar content.

The red clay found at Fiefs Vendeens is primarily composed of limestone and schist, making the soil there very uniform. Because bedrock is so friable, vine roots can quickly take hold and spread.

The history of winemaking here goes back to the Middle Ages, and by the 17th century, Chenin Blanc—also called "Blanc d'Aunis" in Vix or "Franc Blanc" in Brem—was being grown. The two most popular red types at the time were Négrette and Pinot Noir.

In the department, vines grew on 18,000 hectares (44,000 acres) by the 19th century. But as with much of France, the Vendée's grapes had been devastated by phylloxera by the beginning of the 20th century.

Following World War II, growers in all of the subregions competed for approval, and in 1953 the wines were marketed as "Anciens Fiefs du Cardinal" (Cardinal Richelieu had a soft spot for Mareuil wines). Since then, the area has gradually advanced up the appellation ladder, receiving official recognition as "Fiefs Vendéens" in 1965, Vin de Pays status in 1974, VDQS status ("Appellation d'Origine Vin Délimité de Qualité Supérieure") in 1984, and appellation (AOC/AOP) status in 2011.

About half of the wines produced are rosé, with the remaining 30% being red and the remaining 20% being white. There are about 400 hectares (1,000 acres) of vineyards.

Haut-Poitou

The AOC appellation Haut-Poitou is used to identify wines from the Poitiers region in central-western France. The majority of the red, white, and rosé wines included are from Cabernet Sauvignon, Gamay, Cabernet Franc, and Sauvignon Blanc.

Despite being connected to the Loire Valley, the area is still very much an outlying zone. The town at the heart of the appellation, Poitiers, is located a full eighty kilometers (or fifty miles) away from Saumur.

Temperatures are influenced by the ocean, but this region is primarily continental with plenty of sunshine and little annual precipitation (630 mm or 24.8 in). Most soils are chalky.

Vendômois Region

North of Touraine, the lesser-known Vendômois wine district is sometimes lumped in with its more well-known neighbor. There are just three names for it: Jasnières, Côteaux du Loir, and Côteaux du Vendomois. The two main varieties in these areas are Pineau d'Aunis and Chenin Blanc.

Situated at a mean latitude of 47 degrees north, these are some of the northernmost AOCs in France. Only Alsace and Champagne can defeat them.

In addition to its northerly location, there aren't many south-facing slopes for grape ripening. Hence, rather than having deeper notes, wines from the Vendômois are distinguished by their strong acidity and berry-forward aromas.

Wine maps show the district a little off-center because the city of Vendôme is located at its very eastern boundary. This imbalance is further emphasized by the fact that Nantes, Angers, and Tours are neatly located in the center of their respective districts.

The course of the river Loire, not to be mistaken with the larger and more famous Loire, immediately to the south provides a more helpful guide to the form and position of the Vendômois vineyards. The Loir runs 80 kilometers (50 miles) westward to La Flèche after passing through Vendôme. The vineyards of the Vendômois appellations are located on either side of this, especially on the sunnier northern (south facing) banks.

Coteaux du Loir

Just to the north of the Touraine region, in a relatively undiscovered viticultural area, there are 22 communes producing red, white, and rosé wines under the minor appellation coteaux du Loir. As a result, although not being located in the valley, it is categorized as a member of the Loire Valley appellation group.

Vineyards span just over 70 hectares. The title is titled after the path taken by the Loire river. The larger, more well-known Loire should not be confused with this. 35 kilometers (20 miles) south of the latter is located.

Although 35 to 40 percent of the overall output is made up of white wines, wine connoisseurs are most interested in Coteaux du Loir. From extremely sweet, honey-scented botrytized wines to bone dry and steely wines, they range in flavor. Both the growing season's weather and the winemaker have an impact on style.

The Coteaux du Loir whites are made only from Chenin Blanc and have a slight similarity to Vouvray and Savennières and other dry wines. They frequently fall short of these more well-known wines' elegance and richness, though.

This comparison is not as favorable for the whites of the nearby region of Jasnières. They originate in the communes of Ruillé-sur-Loir and L'Homme, from the better-exposed vineyards.

Of the wines produced in the appellation, around 45% are red wines. Pineau d'Aunis, Gamay, Malbec, and "Cabernet," a combination of Franc and Sauvignon, are used to make these. The characteristic of nearly all Loire reds is their fruit-forward style, light body, and moderately high acidity.

Fewer than 20% of Coteaux du Loir wines are rosés. A portion of Grolleau Noir, the grape that has historically produced a large number of delicious Loire rosés, is added to the same varieties that are described above. Out of respect for the Coteaux du Loir appellation, Grolleau is only allowed to make up 25% of blends and is being phased out throughout the Loire.

Coteaux du Loir wines are produced from tuffeau-rich vineyard areas, similar to Saumur to the southwest. When the Loire Valley was completely submerged under the sea 90 million years ago, sedimentary limestone like this was put down.

Coteaux du Vendômois

The appellation Coteaux du Vendômois is used to red, white, and rosé (vin gris) wines produced in 28 parishes located west of the town of Vendôme. In May 2001, it received a promotion from VDQS classification.

Located north of the main vineyard stretch, Coteaux du Vendômois is technically an appellation of the Loire Valley. Situated in Angers, it is a tributary of the Loir (pronounced without a "e"). Located directly downstream of the western boundary are Coteau du Loire et Jasnières.

Given the area's 47 degrees north latitude, it is not unexpected that the wines produced under this appellation are crisp and light. Typically, the scents of berry fruit (found in the reds and rosés) and citrus (found in the whites) predominate over anything earthier and more substantial.

The main ingredient of red Coteaux du Vendômois wines is Pineau d'Aunis, while they can also include traces of Gamay, Cabernet Franc, and Pinot Noir. The most intriguing wines from the district are the vins gris, which are made only from Pineau d'Aunis.

About one bottle out of every six is a white Coteaux du Vendômois wine, which is primarily made of Chenin Blanc with some assistance from Chardonnay. These wines, which are tart and mildly aromatic, are not expected to rival the more intensely flavored Touraine wines, which are located just to the south.

Jasnières

The parishes of Ruillé-sur-Loir and Lhomme are the focal points of the modest white wine appellation known as Jasnières. Situated in the far north of the Loire Valley wine region, it is a subzone of the Coteaux du Loir. You can only use Chenin Blanc.

Depending on the intensity of the winemaker and the circumstances of the growing season, Jasnières wines can be extremely sweet, honey-scented, and botrytized, or bone dry and steely. Although the wines can resemble Vouvray and Savennières to some extent, they are thought to lack the complexity and richness of these more well-known wines. The greatest ones, nevertheless, can continue to look good for at least 15 years.

Jasnières is a subzone of the Coteaux du Loir, but it makes more white wine overall each vintage. An average of 230,000 liters are vinified annually by 20 producers.

Its exceptional terroir is reflected in this volume. Similar to Saumur to the southwest, vineyard locations rich in tuffeau are used to make Jasnieres wines. This limestone was deposited sedimentary 90 million years ago during the Turonian Age, so named because it began when the entire Loire Valley was submerged beneath the sea. The tuffeau decomposes into silica-rich clays in steeper areas.

50 Loire Wine Brand And Regions

1. Domaine de la Romanée-Conti (Sancerre)
2. Pascal Jolivet (Sancerre)
3. Henri Bourgeois (Sancerre)
4. Domaine Vacheron (Sancerre)
5. Domaine Thomas-Labaille (Sancerre)
6. Domaine Reverdy-Ducroux (Sancerre)
7. Domaine Henri Pellé (Menetou-Salon)
8. Domaine des Baumard (Quarts de Chaume)
9. Château de la Ragotière (Muscadet)
10. Domaine de la Pépière (Muscadet)
11. Domaine de la Louvetrie (Muscadet)
12. Domaine Huet (Vouvray)
13. Domaine Vincent Carême (Vouvray)
14. Domaine Marc Brédif (Vouvray)
15. Domaine Guiberteau (Saumur)
16. Bouvet-Ladubay (Saumur)
17. Domaine des Roches Neuves (Saumur-Champigny)
18. Château de Villeneuve (Saumur-Champigny)
19. Domaine Filliatreau (Saumur-Champigny)

20. Domaine des Coutures (Saumur-Champigny)
21. Charles Joguet (Chinon)
22. Domaine Bernard Baudry (Chinon)
23. Couly-Dutheil (Chinon)
24. Domaine Grosbois (Chinon)
25. Domaine de la Chevalerie (Bourgueil)
26. Domaine de la Butte (Bourgueil)
27. Catherine et Pierre Breton (Bourgueil)
28. Domaine de la Chanteleuserie (Bourgueil)
29. Domaine Filliatreau (Bourgueil)
30. Domaine de la Noblaie (Chinon)
31. Domaine Olga Raffault (Chinon)
32. Domaine de la Grange Tiphaine (Montlouis-sur-Loire)
33. Domaine François Chidaine (Montlouis-sur-Loire)
34. Domaine La Taille aux Loups (Montlouis-sur-Loire)
35. Domaine de Bellivière (Jasnières)
36. Domaine de Closel (Savennières)
37. Domaine FL (Jasnieres)
38. Domaine Richou (Anjou)

39. Domaine du Closel (Savennières)
40. Domaine des Baumard (Savennières)
41. Domaine de Bablut (Quincy)
42. Domaine Pellé (Menetou-Salon)
43. Domaine Mardon (Quincy)
44. Domaine de Reuilly (Reuilly)
45. Domaine Fouassier (Sancerre)
46. Domaine de la Taille aux Loups (Montlouis-sur-Loire)
47. Domaine Guion (Bourgueil)
48. Domaine des Roches Neuves (Saumur-Champigny)
49. Domaine du Salvard (Cheverny)
50. Domaine de la Châtaigneraie (Touraine)

Loire Wine And Their Food Pairing

Sancerre (Sauvignon Blanc):

Pair with goat cheese, oysters, grilled asparagus, or seafood dishes.

Vouvray (Chenin Blanc):

Complements rich dishes like creamy poultry, lobster, or Thai cuisine.

Chinon (Cabernet Franc):

Matches well with roasted meats, grilled vegetables, and charcuterie.

Muscadet (Melon de Bourgogne):

Ideal with oysters, clams, mussels, and light seafood.

Saumur (Chenin Blanc or Cabernet Franc):

Chenin Blanc pairs well with pork dishes, while Cabernet Franc complements roasted meats.

Bourgueil (Cabernet Franc):

Goes well with lamb, grilled meats, and hearty stews.

Quincy (Sauvignon Blanc):

Pair with salads, light appetizers, or goat cheese.

Vouvray (Sparkling):

Great with sushi, fried foods, or as an aperitif.

Anjou (Chenin Blanc or Cabernet Franc):

Chenin Blanc works with rich poultry, while Cabernet Franc pairs with roasted meats.

Cheverny (Sauvignon Blanc/Chardonnay blend):

Versatile; pairs with salads, seafood, and light chicken dishes.

Montlouis-sur-Loire (Chenin Blanc):
Complements spicy foods, Asian cuisine, and creamy cheeses.

Jasnieres (Chenin Blanc):
Pairs well with seafood, shellfish, and light poultry dishes.

Savennières (Chenin Blanc):
Matches well with roasted chicken, pork, and creamy sauces.

Reuilly (Sauvignon Blanc or Pinot Noir):
Sauvignon Blanc pairs with salads and seafood, while Pinot Noir complements poultry.

Menetou-Salon (Sauvignon Blanc or Pinot Noir):
Sauvignon Blanc works with grilled fish, while Pinot Noir pairs with game or pork.

Touraine (Various Varieties):

Pair Sauvignon Blanc with salads, goat cheese, and light seafood.

Gamay and Cabernet Franc work well with charcuterie and grilled meats.

Quarts de Chaume (Chenin Blanc - Sweet):

Enjoy with foie gras, blue cheese, or fruity desserts.

Montlouis-sur-Loire (Sparkling):

Ideal for brunch with pastries, fresh fruit, and creamy cheeses.

Saumur-Champigny (Cabernet Franc):

Pairs beautifully with grilled lamb, pork, and hearty stews.

Coteaux du Layon (Chenin Blanc - Sweet):

Perfect with desserts like apple pie, caramel, or blue cheese.

Pouilly-Fumé (Sauvignon Blanc):
Compliments goat cheese, smoked salmon, and light pasta dishes.

Château de Villeneuve (Saumur-Champigny):
Ideal with grilled meats, game, and rustic French cuisine.

Domaine des Baumard (Quarts de Chaume):
Enjoy with rich desserts like crème brûlée or fruit tarts.

Domaine de la Pépière (Muscadet):
Pair with raw oysters, shrimp, or other fresh seafood.

Charles Joguet (Chinon):
Complements beef, lamb, and grilled vegetables.

Domaine Richou (Anjou):
Pairs well with poultry, pork, and light vegetarian dishes.

Domaine des Coutures (Saumur-Champigny):
Ideal with grilled meats, sausages, and charcuterie.

Domaine Olga Raffault (Chinon):
Complements roasted meats, game, and hearty stews.

Domaine de la Noblaie (Chinon):
Pairs well with grilled meats, mushrooms, and aged cheeses.

Domaine de la Butte (Bourgueil):
Ideal with charcuterie, grilled sausages, and game.

Domaine Guiberteau (Saumur):
Pair with roasted chicken, veal, and dishes with cream-based sauces.

Bouvet-Ladubay (Saumur):

Ideal as an aperitif and pairs well with sushi and light seafood.

Domaine de la Louvetrie (Muscadet):

Perfect with raw oysters, clams, and grilled fish.

Domaine La Taille aux Loups (Montlouis-sur-Loire):

Complements spicy Asian dishes, creamy cheeses, and poultry.

Domaine François Chidaine (Montlouis-sur-Loire):

Pairs well with grilled lobster, creamy pasta, and light seafood.

Domaine de Bellivière (Jasnières):

Ideal with shellfish, crab, and creamy goat cheese.

Domaine de Closel (Savennières):

Perfect with roast chicken, lobster, and rich, creamy sauces.

Domaine FL (Jasnieres):

Pairs well with grilled shrimp, chicken dishes, and light salads.

Domaine de Bablut (Quincy):

Ideal with salads, goat cheese, and light vegetarian dishes.

Domaine Pellé (Menetou-Salon):

Complements grilled fish, seafood, and light pasta dishes.

Domaine Mardon (Quincy):

Pairs well with shellfish, grilled vegetables, and fresh salads.

Domaine de Reuilly (Reuilly):

Ideal with grilled chicken, seafood, and light appetizers.

Domaine des Roches Neuves (Saumur-Champigny):
Complements grilled lamb, beef, and hearty stews.

Domaine du Salvard (Cheverny):
Pairs well with salads, light pasta, and fresh seafood.

Domaine de la Châtaigneraie (Touraine):
Ideal with grilled sausages, pork, and charcuterie.

Printed in Dunstable, United Kingdom